# The Novels of Anita Desai

## A Study in Character and Conflict

**About the Book**

Anita Desai is the foremost Indian novelist of the post-Independence era. She has been awarded the prestigious Sahitya Akademi Award for the novel *Fire on the Mountain* and Authors' Guild Award for Excellence in Writing for *Where Shall We Go This Summer?* A close reading of her novels reveals that her real concern is with the exploration of human psyche. The present book is the first study of its kind that assesses Anita Desai's characters in the light of Third Force Psychology. Drawing its concepts of neurotic processes from Karen Horney and its understanding of health from the tenets of Abraham Maslow, this study probes the real self of various characters and tries to ascertain their intrinsic nature.

**About the Author**

Dr. Usha Bande was Head, Department of English, Govt. Girls College, Shimla. An eminent scholar and perceptive critic, she has had a brilliant academic career. She studied at St. Joseph's Convent, Jabalpur; Punjab University, Chandigarh; and H.P. University, Shimla. She has published the books *Mothers and Mother-Figures in Indo-English Literature*, *Victim Consciousness in Indian English Novel* and several scholarly papers in India and abroad.

ISBN: 81-85218-01-3

# The Novels of Anita Desai

## A Study in Character and Conflict

Usha Bande

Prestige Books International
New Delhi

*Published by*
**Prestige Books International**
New Delhi 110 060
prestigebooks@gmail.com
Phone: 9818755529

*Associate Office*
50, Clapham Common Westside
London SW 49 A S, U.K.

*Associate Office*
P.O. Box 2250, Sydney 2001


Edition 2018
ISBN: 81-85218-01-3



Printed in India

# Contents

# PREFACE

Fascinated by *Fire on the Mountain* and again by *Clear Light of Day*, I felt increasingly drawn by the writings of Anita Desai; aware though that her novels are by no means "light reading." A close reading of other works revealed that Desai's real concern is with exploration of human psyche. I realised that her forte lay in her characters—unusual, neurotic but not ready to accept life as it came. Her writings reveal inner realities and psychic reverberations of her characters.

The realisation led me to a study of her characters in the light of Third Force psychology. Drawing its concepts of neurotic processes from Karen Horney and its understanding of health from the tenets of Abraham Maslow, this study probes the "real self" of various characters and tries to ascertain their intrinsic nature. The attempt is to find out when and how they get alienated from their real self and if it has been possible for them to regain their normal health.

I cannot close these prefatory remarks without expressing my gratitude to those who have been kind enough to help me in the preparation of this project. I feel indebted to my learned supervisor Dr. Atma Ram, Principal, Govt. Post-graduate College, Dharamsala, for his unfailing help, affection and guidance. My special thanks go to the renowned scholar Dr. B.J. Paris, Professor of English, Florida University, U.S.A., who in his works makes exposition of literature in the light of

Third Force psychology. Dr. Paris was considerate enough to send me articles, research papers and books pertaining to the present study. I owe him suggestions that have been of inestimable value to me.

My thanks are also due to Dr. R.K. Dhawan, University of Delhi, who read the manuscript and gave valuable suggestions; to my friend Mrs. Shashi Kanta who was always forthcoming in extending me help; to my mother Mrs. Sushila Bande who was a constant source of inspiration; to my father Mr. M.R. Bande who scrupulously checked the text of every quotation and compared it with the original; to Mr. Gajinder Choudhary for seeing through the production of the book.

USHA BANDE

*For My Parents*

*M.R. Bande and Sushila Bande*

# ABBREVIATIONS

| | |
|---|---|
| *CP* | *Cry, the Peacock* |
| *VC* | *Voices in the City* |
| *BBB* | *Bye-Bye, Blackbird* |
| *FOM* | *Fire on the Mountain* |
| *WSGS* | *Where Shall We Go This Summer ?* |
| *CLD* | *Clear Light of Day* |
| *IC* | *In Custody* |
| *GAT* | *Games at Twilight* |
| *NHG* | *Neurosis and Human Growth* |
| *NPT* | *The Neurotic Personality of Our Time* |
| *MP* | *Motivation and Personality* |
| *TPB* | *Towards a Psychology of Being* |

# 1

# INTRODUCTION

Anita Desai is one of the most serious yet appealing novelists on the Indian-English firmament. Her reputation has been steadily rising since the publication of her first novel, *Cry, the Peacock* (1963). Whereas Arun Joshi's works show a rich note of social realism, Raji Narasimhan's that of the plight of the liberated woman, Anita Desai's novels unravel the mystery of the inner life of her characters. Her works are different from those of other Indian women writers in English: Nayantara Sahgal, Kamala Markandaya, and Ruth Prawer Jhabvala, who mainly concern themselves with politics, East-West encounter and social themes respectively. Anita Desai is interested in the psychic life of her characters. For her it is "depth which is interesting, delving deeper and deeper in a character or a scene rather than going round about it."[1] She incorporates themes such as the agony of existence, the metaphysical void, the fears and tremblings of her protagonists whose values, beliefs and structures are jeopardized, which, in turn, stand in the way of the individual's self-realization. However, there is a genuine attempt suggesting a struggle to attain a maturity of outlook, and positive growth. Her forte is "the exploration of sensibility—the particular kind of Indian sensibility that is ill at ease among barbarians and the philistines, the anarchists and the amoralists."[2]

Since the publication of her first novel, Anita Desai has received substantial critical acclaim. Her works have elicited five full-length studies besides quite a few articles and essays. Her marked edge derives from the richness of her narrative technique and the vast extension of the inner world that imparts a problematic and elusive nature to her writings. As early as 1971 Meena Belliappa discussed the scope and nature of her first two novels and found in her "evidence of a departure from current modes of fictional writing and of an earnest effort to break new grounds."[3] R.S. Sharma refers to her "anti-fiction" and considers her a "novelist of moods, of persistent states of mind and psyche."[4] For him, through Maya's tragedy, the novelist weaves social fatalism into a coherent pattern to communicate the tender sensibility of a woman. Anita Desai disowns all social concerns and asserts more than once that she is interested in individuals and not in social issues. Social issues intrude only where they affect the characters.

Madhusudan Prasad[5] considers her a grassroot existentialist. In her lyricism, he spots the themes of nausea, boredom and the human condition. In an interview with Yashodhara Dalmia, the novelist also admits of her preoccupation with the "essential human condition." Indeed, almost all the thematic studies of her novels have concentrated on loneliness and withdrawal of her characters—be it self-imposed like that of Nanda Kaul or Sita, or circumstantial as that of Bim or Monisha. B. Ramachandra Rao[6] examines the poetic texture and rich imagination of the novelist, and the lyric sensitivity of her personages, in her four novels. He finds an interaction between poetic texture and the narrative structure. Jasbir Jain's *Stairs to the Attic: The Novels of Anita Desai* views her works thematically, bringing out in the process her psychological concerns. According to her, the "warp and woof" of her works attracts attention when "the themes are analysed, the social and political elements are subtly camouflaged and subdued by dwelling on emotions and responses which are far more engrossing than the hard facts of reality."[7] As her discussion progresses from thematic concerns to philosophical and psychological issues, Jain's study reveals the powerful feminist trends in Anita Desai.

The approach to evaluate her works in relation to the general trends and achievements of Indo-English writings as a whole is gaining popularity. Many critics appreciate her uniquely Indian sensitivity, while several others view her fiction on the national canvas. Charmazel Dult's approach to *Where Shall We Go This Summer ?*[8] for example, is based on relating Sita's desperate search for direction to India's anxiety to find her identity after her newly-acquired freedom. Some readers study the theme of racial alienation in *Bye-Bye, Blackbird* (1971). R.S. Singh considers it a "weak variation on the theme of racial arrogance." Meenakshi Mukherjee observes that the theme of rootlessness is a part of that vital experience which is attracting the attention of many Indian writers. She makes a comparative study of Kamala Markandaya's *Nowhere Man*, and Anita Desai's *Bye-Bye Blackbird*, and feels that loss of ego is a humiliating experience of the immigrant situation.[10] Comparative studies of East-West encounters in Indo-English novels yield a variety of treatment given to the possibility and prospects of establishing meaningful relationships between two racial and cultural groups. In Anita Desai's novels one can trace a symbolic representation of the equality of status achieved by India after her independence. Here, the male lover is Indian who wooes and weds a white woman in her own country.

Another recurrent pattern in criticism is to focus on the artist's search for his literary nationality. *Bye-Bye, Blackbird* embodies the quest for philosophical and sociological identity. G. P. Sharma[11] seeks to reject the view that Indian English literature is far removed form the soil. Sharma opines that it sufficiently mirrors the nationalist spirit of India. The *Karma* theory running through the entire narrative of *Cry, the Peacock* and the depiction of woman's plight in modern Indian society in Desai's novels confirm the fact that modern Indian woman's psychic turmoil reveals an era of awakening.

There is also a trend to evaluate Anita Desai as a woman through her own reflections and comments. Since very scanty biorgaphical material is available on her, some scholars analyse the idealism and commitments of her fictional characters, and apply them to the personality of their creator. B.O. Vyas, for example, sees her as a perfectionist, having faith in life and individuality. That she has faith in life is attested by her own statement, though made in a different context. She affirms: if one opts for life one must compromise with it, like Sita, in *Where Shall We Go This Summer ?* According to her "drawing a line means certain death."[12] One should learn, like Sita, to be a part of the earth and of life. These views can further be testified by her characters's search for life. Dharma in *Voices in the City* (1965) is an artist who turns away temporarily from human society, but feels unfulfilled until he paints a human portrait. In her interview with Keṭaki Sheth, the novelist points out: "To a novelist it is always the individual who is of primary interest and not the anonymous multitude, always the particular rather than the general."[13] She, however, believes that one cannot draw a rigid line between masculine and feminine styles and judge the creator. It is just a matter of placing emphasis differently. "Seen in this light James had the most exquisitelv feminine style—D.H. Lawrence was extraordinarily 'feminine' too. These differences in the male and female styles will even out as the differences in their lives disapppear."[14] In the fictional world of Desai the creed is the value of the individual and individualism.

## II

From the survey of the critical material on Anita Desai's fiction done on the preceding pages, it transpires that critics and scholars have largely dwelt on the thematic and philosophical aspects of her writings. Her skill in characterization has received but scant attention. As a writer, interested in the individual only—whether men or women, young or old or children—Anita Desai displays a great creative ability. Being a novelist of moods and the state of psyche, her characters have a tendency to turn inward. *Cry, the Peacock* (1963) is the story of a hypersensitive young woman Maya, pitted against a taciturn husband. She lives a life of acute sensitivity and dies in her quest to find fuller life. The novelist employs an apt symbol of a lamp extinguished because of too much of oil that "drowned the wick."[15] In *Voices in the City*[16] (1965), the three major characters—Nirode, Amla and Monisha—undergo existential crises. They are questers, looking for a proper vocation. Nirode strives to find life in self-abnegation, Monisha searches it in privacy, and both fail. Amla turns to art and realises that losing one's self is not an answer to life. *Bye-Bye, Blackbird*[17] (1971) deals with the psychic turmoil of Sarah who struggles to find her identity. *Where Shall We Go This Summer?*[18] (1975) is the story of a near-neurotic heroine, Sita. She wishes to escape the mundane reality of her existence in a bid to discover peace in her childhood home, but finally compromises with life as it is. *Fire on the Mountain*[19] (1977) incorporates the story of Nanda Kaul and her great grand-daughter Raka. Nanda flees life only to realise that one is always entangled in the past. *Clear Light of Day*[20] (1980) is the story of Bim who, after a long period of frustration and anger, comes to recognise the importance of an attitude; to forget and forgive. *In Custody*[21] (1984), Anita Desai's latest novel, shows a significant broadening of her views. The story is woven round an idea: the failure of Deven Sharma to get an interview with Nur Sahjehanbadi. He is deceived and trapped, yet at long last he is able to separate art from life and feel "whole" despite his shattering experiences.

Anita Desai's characters can be classified in two distinctive groups—those who fail to adjust to the harsh realities of life and those who compromise. The premise which provides the momentum to her creative activity is the "basic human condition." In a novel, as in life, there are those who always remain "outsiders" because they cannot accommodate themselves to the world of realities. Tennessee Williams distinguishes between those persons who adopt themselves to this world and those who suffer under a sense of personal inadequacy. He characterizes the latter as "outsiders" and points out that the artists and the insane fall under this slot. With them he groups those who are neither artists nor lunatics but have elements of lunacy or vision. These people also remain "outsiders" as they can never be a part of this world. We encounter some such characters in Anita Desai's world. In order to describe their illusions, fantasies and fabrications, Anita Desai discards the traditional, worn-out realism and diverts her attention to the disintegrating forces in their inner and outer lives. Her view of truth and reality, as "nine-tenth of the iceberg that submerged beneath one-tenth visible portion we call Reality,"[22] gives a definite shape to her vision of life and constitutes the basis of her philosophical doctrine.

The question of presenting real characters has been approached by different critics. Mary McCarthy believes that modern writers do not give us the kind of real people that live in the works of Tolstoy and Dickens. She points out that the "real people" in novels are not the heroes or heroines, but the minor characters who do not change. W.J. Harvey, on the other hand, maintains that the changeless personages are "Card" characters. They are merely the result of the novelist "forcing us to take an outside" or objective view of them. Though the joy of their character lies in the immunity to the blows of life, they are not a part of the empirical reality. The difference between their realism and that of the protagonists is one of quality. Card-like characters are "chemically pure" but, "their realism is one of intensity, singleness, vivacity; the realism of the protagonist is that of dilution, complexity and process."[23] For Harvey, the realist novelists exhibit a passion for life which can over-ride the formal nature of their art. As a result, form suffers at the hands of characters. Harvey complains that the New Criticism has failed to deal with characterization as it is engaged in the elaboration of imagery, symbolism and the structure of a work of art. He terms it the "retreat from character."

Recent trends in literary criticism enable us to see a character as central to a realistic novel, having only a mimetic function. B.J. Paris thinks that fictional characters can be understood as real people: "A careful examination of the nature of realistic fiction, as modern criticism is coming to conceive it, will show that in certain cases it is proper to treat literary characters as real people and that by doing so can we fully appreciate the distinctive achievement of the genre."[24] In a realistic novel, the author is mainly concerned with the representation of his characters, not interpretation. This is what Northrop Frye calls "the low-mimetic function of art." In the modern context, reality does not mean social reality because social reality is a changing phenomenon. Bernard Bergonzi observes that the traditional way of conceiving a character has altered completely because the concept of reality now is different: ". . . the change arising from the decline of religious or metaphysical certainties, the influence of modern psychology, and the public crimes and traumas of the twentieth century."[25] The hero or the heroine is no longer absolute and invulnerable in modern fiction but rather insecure, apprehensive, inward-looking and brooding, conveying the daily pains involved in the act of living.

The varieties of conceptions of reality as they exist in literature vary with different writers and critics. Virginia Woolf equates reality with life and observes that human nature, which is life, is actuality. The developmental forces of history and social organization are Erich Auerbach's reality. For Ian Watt, it is time, self-consciousness and language. Anita Desai achieves the sense of reality by probing the innermost depths of human psyche. This provides her a theme which runs like a thread all through her works from *Cry, the Peacock* to *In Custody*: the wholeness to which all other concepts of loneliness, escape, detachment, time, death and conflicts are subordinated. True to this assertion, life itself becomes a quest, as Suno, one of the characters says, "life has taken a different path for me, in the form of a search, not a race."[26] Life is a perpetual search and "the terror of facing single-handed the ferocious assaults of existence,"[27] is the fundamental reality of life. The novelist regards the world as something "ethereal," much in the same way as Virginia Woolf considers life a "luminous halo, a semi-transparent envelop surrounding us from the beginning of consciousness to the end,"[28] or as Henry James believes, that man has a yearning to live as the great truth above life, or as Somerset Maugham holds, man is engaged in a constant search to free himself from bondage.

Anita Desai seeks to discover and convey through her characters, the significance of things by delving deep down the mysteries of the mind. As she asserts:

> My writing is an effort to discover, underline and convey the significance of things. I must seize upon that incomplete

> and seemingly meaningless mass of reality around me and try and discover its significance by plunging below the surface and plumbing the depths, then illuminating those depths till they become more lucid, brilliant and explicable reflection of the visible world.[29]

This approach to the "visible world" is essentially subjective. Anita Desai portrays, not the experience of the external object, but the cognizance of objective reality as seen by the mind. Here she comes closer to Henry James's view of reality as the very "experience," the atmosphere of the mind. Her struggle with reality is, in a certain sense, an effort to define it. To reach this, she captures the sensations, feelings and emotions of her characters in the flux of the world. That is why her personages, in novels as well as in short stories, are unique individuals having their secret inner lives. Like the Greeks, they wish to preserve "the idea of beauty, harmony, and complete human perfection, so present and paramount."[30] Some of them like Sita in *Where Shall We Go This Summer ?* and Suno in the short story "Studies in the Park" find it revealed in the vision of love. It is a love "so intense. Divine or insane." (*GAT*, p. 30) For others, the moments of revelation of life come in an aesthetic experience, such as the grandeur of early morning flight of pigeons seen by Mr. Bosu in "Pigeons at Daybreak," or in the manifestation of natural beauty as in *In Custody*, when the sky fills in with a grey light and the pampas grass "waved in a sudden breeze that had sprung up, laughing, waving and rustling through the grasses with a live, rippling sound." (*IC* p. 204)

As an artist, Anita Desai handles the raw material of life and conveys it through a pattern and design. Writing itself is a quest for meaning, for value and for truth. She is as much interested in life, with its hopes, frustrations, negations, rejections and the chaotic flow of events, as she is concerned with art to give shape, purpose and wholeness to life. Fiedler believes that a creative work starts with the interaction of man and life. "Artistic activity begins when man finds himself face to face with the visible world as with something immensely enigmatical. . . . In the creation of a work of art, man, engaged in a struggle with nature not for his physical but for his mental existence."[31] Indeed, life and art cannot be separated. Life provides the matter, that is, the reality of lived experience, around which Anita Desai's characters are woven. They are peculiar and eccentric. To accept life as it comes in routine is a sign of averageness, and Anita Desai refuses to see her creations in the light of mediocrity. They are individuals with the force of personality to say "Yes" or "No." The novelist affirms in an interview:

> I am interested in characters who are not average but have retreated, or been driven into despair and so turned against or made to stand against the general current. It is easy to flow with the current, it makes no demands, it costs no efforts. But those who cannot follow it, whose heart cries out 'the great No,' who fight the current and struggle against it, they know what demands are and what it costs to meet them.[32]

That is why her protagonists have defiant individuality. They fight against the commonplace conformity and stick to their own vision of life. Those who manage to say the "Great No" and yet grow independent of their environment are saved from a total disaster. Others who say "No" but do not find the positive way to unburden their "self," are entangled in their own introspection, failing, thus, to revivify their strength.

It is an empirical reality that the centre of each realm of experience is always the Self. And since no centre can exist without its ultimate organic periphery, the experience which originates with the human mind at its core, requires the objective amplification of reality. If reality is what Leon Edel calls "a synthesis of the thing perceived and the perceiving subject,"[33] the preceiving subject is the consciousness of her protagonists. Concerned with the subjective analysis, Anita Desai shifts her attention to the inner sensibilities. With the help of outer conditions she reveals the inner workings of her characters. So vividly portrayed are their introspection and mood-swings that a pertinent question is often posed if her characterization is autobiographical, to which her reply is, that minor characters, incidents and settings have personal bearings to some extent and are based on experience. But, the major characters and their eccentricities are imaginary or an amalgamation of several characters from real life. "My characters are composites, they're hybrid really. I find that I sometimes use a minor character just as I found him but I've never taken the major characters in my books from life—only certain features and characteristics, not all."[34] Here, one is reminded of André Gide's assertion that an author does not always reveal himself in his personages:

> It is rare that an author who reveals himself in a novel produces a character who resembles him, that is to say, a living human individual. . . . The authentic novelist creates his characters with the infinite possibilities his life may hold; the false novelist creates them along the single line of his factual experience. The genius of the novel brings the possible to life; it is not simply a copy of the actual.[35]

Anita Desai's characters reveal her vision of life; they share her perceptions, and they set out in quest of meaning. Like their creator they love solitude and privacy.

Preoccupation with the psyche of her men, women and childern diverts Desai's attention to the nausea of existence. The complexities of her writing emanate from her existential roots and impart it a tangible form. But fortunately, for her characters existence is not wholly irredeemable. The panacea, for most of them, lies in the aesthetics of life.

Her critical portraits: hypersensitive Maya; lonely Monisha; rebellious Nirode; bored Sita; discarded Nanda; peculiar Raka; sensitive but balanced Bim; and simple Deven—all provide a vast potential for a psycho-analytical study. These characters pass through a state of psychological crises damaging their value system. Some of them are lost, while some get out of their alienation. A psychological analysis will enable us to amplify their conflicts, understand their behaviour and know them as human beings.

## NOTES

1. Jasbir Jain, "Anita Desai: Interviewed." *Rajasthan University Studies in English*, 12 (1979), pp. 61-69.
2. K.R.S. Iyengar, *Indian Writing in English* (1963: rpt. New Delhi: Sterling, 1983), p. 464.
3. Meena Belliappa, *Anita Desai: A Study of her Fiction* (Calcutta: Writers' Workshop, 1971), p. 1.
4. R.S. Sharma, *Anita Desai* (New Delhi: Arnold Heinemann, 1983), p. 166.
5. Madhusudan Prasad, *Anita Desai: The Novelist* (Allahabad: New Horizon, 1981).
6. B. Ramachandra Rao, *The Novels of Anita Desai* (New Delhi: Kalyani, 1977).
7. Jasbir Jain, *Stairs to the Attic: The Novels of Anita Desai* (Jaipur: Printwell, 1987), p. 1.
8. Charmazel Dult, "Past and Present: A Journey to Confrontation," *The Journal of Indian Writing in English*, vol. 9. (Jan. 1981), pp. 67-73. This is a special Anita Desai Number. It contains nine papers focusing on structure, themes, motifs, symbols and technique of her art.
9. R.S. Singh, "Facets of Consciousness in Recent Indo-English Novel," in K.K. Sharma, ed., *Indo-English Literature* (Ghaziabad: Vimal, 1977), p. 232.
10. Meenakshi Mukherjee, "The Theme of Displacement in Anita Desai and Kamala Markandaya," *World Literature Written in English*, Vol. 17, No. 1, April 1978, pp. 225-35.
11. G.P. Sarma, *Nationalism in Indo-Anglian Fiction* (New Delhi: Sterling, 1978).
12. Atma Ram, "Interview with Anita Desai," in *Interviews with Indian Writers* (Calcutta Writers' Workshop, 1983), pp. 21-33.
13. Ketaki Sheth, "It's Fatal to Write with an audience in Mind," Interview in *Imprint*. June 1984, pp. 58-63,

14. Anita Desai, "Women Writers," *Quest*, April-June, 1970, p. 42.

15. Anita Desai, *Cry, the Peacock* (New Delhi: Hind Pocket Books, 1963).

16. Anita Desai, *Voices in the City* (New Delhi: Orient Paperbacks, 1968).

17. Anita Desai, *Bye-Bye, Blackbird* (New Delhi: Orient Paperbacks, 1971).

18. Anita Desai, *Where Shall We Go this Summer?* (1975; rpt. Orient Paperbacks, 1982).

19. Anita Desai, *Fire on the Mountain* (New Delhi: Allied, 1977).

20. Anita Desai, *Clear Light of Day* (New Delhi: Allied, 1980).

21. Anita Desai, *In Custody* (London: Heinemann, 1984).

22. Yashodhara Dalmia, "An Interview with Anita Desai," *The Times of India*, 29 April 1979, p. 4.

23. W.H. Harvey, *Character and the Novel* (New York: Ithaca, 1965), pp. 187-88.

24. Bernard J. Paris, *A Psychological Approach to Fiction* (Bloomington: Indiana University Press, 1974), p.4.

25. Bernard Bergonzi, *The Situation of the Novel* (London: Macmillan, 1970), p. 36.

26. Anita Desai, "Studies in the Park," *Games at Twilight* (Harmondsworth: Penguin, 1978), p. 32.

27. Ortega Y. Gasset, quoted by Anita Desai in "An Interview" in *The Times of India*, p. 4.

28. Virginia Woolf, *Modern Fiction* (1919; rpt. London: Hogarth, 1929), p. 189.

29. Anita Desai, "Replies to the Questionnaire," *Kakatiya Journal of English Studies*, 3, No.1, 1978, pp. 1-6.

30. Matthew Arnold, *Culture and Anarchy*, ed. J. Dover Wilson (Cambridge: University Press, 1971), p. 55.

31. Conrad Fiedler, *On Judging Works of Visual Art*, trans. Henry Schafer-Simmer and Fuller Mood (Berkeley: University of California Press, 1949), p. 48.

32. Atma Ram, "Interview," pp. 22-33.

33. Leon Edel, *The Psychological Novel: 1900-1950* (London: Rupert Hart-Davis, 1955), p. 129.

34. Ketaki Sheth, "Interview," *Imprint, pp.* 58-63.

35. André Gide, *Journal des Faux-Monnayeurs* (Paris: Gallimard, 1927), p. 96. Quoted by Enrico Garzilli in *Circles Without Centre* (Massachusetts: Harvard University Press, 1972), p. 119.

# 2

# THIRD FORCE AND LITERARY CHARACTERS

Freud, during his studies, often maintained that the credit of discovering the unconscious goes to the poets and philosophers before him, and that he simply discovered the scientific method by which the unconscious could be studied. J. C. Ransom, an admirer of Freud, asserted the master's views and said as far back as 1924, that psycho-analysis is not a new tèchnique; poets and writers have always accepted it as "gospel truth." It is, in fact, " the systematic or scientific application of technique that poets and artists have generally been aware of."[1] Since literature is a vision of life of the artist, seeing the multiplicity and complexity of mind, its subjectivity and interiority, the affinity between literature and psycho-analysis cannot be challenged.

Literature and psychology, put together, can benefit the students of both these faculties. Psychologists uncover and discuss the various phenomena of human psyche; literary artists amplify them by concrete portrayal. What psychologists put forth in theories, literary artists convey through artistic presention, with the help of intuition. Indeed, literature as well as life reveal those recesses of human mind that are beyond conscious understanding. Karen Horney also makes frequent references to literary characters and observes that great writers have grasped psychological phenomenon intuitively and "have presented it in impressive forms than a psychiatrist can hope to do."[2] B. J. Paris, an exponent in the use of Third Force Psychology for literary and cultural criticism, agrees that realistic fiction can be understood better if we analyse mimetic characters psychologically. He finds psycho-analytical criticism valuable for the explication of a fictional character as well as the implied author. He observes that even if we cannot accept the implied author's values as adequate to his fictional world, "we have a marvellously rich portrayal of a particular kind of consciousness making ethical responses to a variety of human situations."[3]

Third Force psychology is not a new branch of psychology. It comprises a group of Neo-Freudians, Neo-Jungians, Gestalt Therapists, Existential and Humanistic psychologists.[4] What they have in common is their belief that man is not a conditioned animal, but he has in him a third force which is "evolutionary constructive." Every human being has an intrinsic nature. It is neither wholly good, nor wholly bad, is rather neutral and weak. It can be pressurized by habit, cultural and social forces, but it cannot be eliminated altogether. It remains with man forever and struggles for self-actualization. If this "inner nature" is suppressed one gets sick, if it is encouraged, it leads to a healthy personality. Thus, Third Force psychologists give us clues to self-actualization and self-alienation. The two leading spokesmen are Abraham Masfow and Karen Horney. The picture of a balanced growth, given by Maslow and the concepts of self-alienation propounded by Karen Horney have provided us critical norms to judge constructive and destructive behaviour. A book, says Roger Fry, is "the direct outcome of an apprehension of some emotion of actual life."[5] In a novel, the conflicts, complexes, defences and the working of the inner life of characters can be studied in the light of Third Force concepts of health or sickness. Since these theories are not commonly used as yet, I devote some space to an exposition of Third Force.

The explanatory and synchronic character of Third Force psychology offers a sophisticated picture of human nature. Karen Horney's concept of "basic anxiety" and Abraham Maslow's theory of "basic needs" provide a systematic analysis of the evolutionary nature of man. Horney describes basic anxiety as the "feeling of being isloated and helpless in a world conceived as potentially hostile." (*NHG*, p.18) These feelings arise in childhood when one does not get favourable conditions to grow according to his individual needs. Children whose parents do not give them genuine love, lose the sense of belonging, the "we" feeling, and develop "profound insecurity and vague apprehensiveness." (*NHG*, p.18) Unconditional love is essential for the healthy growth of a child. Many factors hamper the flow of warmth and affection. Dominating, over-protective, intimidating, irritable, over-indulgent, partial, indifferent, hypocritical elders endanger a child's free use of his energies, damage his sense of self-esteem and self-reliance. He cannot relate himself to others with his spontaneous real self. Consequently, he develops some strategy to copy with his environment and unconsciously diverts his constructive energies towards alleviating his basic anxiety.

Erich Fromm also recognises the importance of "relatedness" and the dread of isolation. He describes the emergence of individuation as the process of "growing aloneness." with the physical emotional growth of the child, his will develops. A child severs his primary ties and becomes independent. This is a delicate period of his life as he feels powerless, insecure and isolated because the sense of security offered by primary ties is suddenly withdrawn from him and he becomes aware of himself as a separate entity. The result of this anxiety can be twofold. A child may submerge himself in the outside world and give in to hostile feelings or he may develop in a productive way and may establish a spontaneous relationship with man and nature. "If every step in the direction of separation and individuation were matched by corresponding growth of the self, the development of the child would be harmonious."[6] But, while individuation is an automatic process, growth of self is affected by various social and personal factors. The child who develops harmoniously acquires a healthy personality.

Abraham Maslow's theory of the hierarchy of basic needs also emphasises on man's fundamental desire to "belong." According to him, all have psychological survival needs which include need for safety, for love, for belonging, for self-esteem and finally for self-actualization. These are arranged in an order of hierarchy. The most basic of them is the safety need. Once a child feels safe and secure, he grows into a healthy child. Thereafter come the feelings of belonging, of love. These lead to self-esteem. Once the fundamental need is fulfilled, other needs go on arising till a human being reaches self-actualization. Maslow feels that the needs at the upper end of the hierarchy are weak and depend on the gratification of the lower needs. He, therefore, postulates that man is an evolutionary creature whose higher nature seeks actualization just as surely as does his lower nature. Sickness arises when this upward evolution is blocked. "This higher nature includes the need for meaningful work, for responsibility, for creativeness, for being fair and just, for doing what is worthwhile and for preferring to do it well."[7] This is in contrast to man's lower nature, which seeks gratification of the animal instincts. However, all these needs are basic in the sense that they are integral to his biological nature. Man's values, desires and fantasies are focused on his strongest unmet need. Frustration of these produces neurotic conditions. His growth is arrested; he is alienated from his real self.

Both Maslow and Horney regard "real self" as the foundation of personality, the "central inner force, common to all human beings and yet unique in each." Under favourable conditions, an individual will develop his potentialities. As Horney observes, these are

> . . . the unique alive forces of his real self: the clarity and depth of his own feelings, thoughts, wishes, interest; the ability to tap his own resources, the strength of his will power; the special capacities or gifts he may have; the faculty to express himself to others with his spontaneous feelings. All this will in time enable him to find his set of values and his aims in life. (*NHG*, p.17)

Given favourable environment, warmth of affection, inner security and inner freedom, the child learns to live according to his real self. Maslow considers real self weak. A child's urge for safety, warmth and love are so strong that he can abandon his real self if these psychological needs are at stake: "The primary choice is between others and one's own self. If the only way to maintain the self is to lose the other, then the ordinary child will give up the self." (*TPB*, p. 50) Neurosis begins when the real self is forsaken.

Basic anxiety produces in a child, what Maslow calls, "basic threat." His basic needs are frustrated and he dreads the environment which is merciless and unfair to him. As a result of this fear, his attitude towards himself and his environment changes. He becomes self-protective and relates himself to others not by his real self but by compulsive drives. His likes, dislikes, wants and wishes, trust and distrust are all governed by strategic necessities. According to Horney, "he cannot simply like or dislike, trust or distrust, express his wishes or protest against those of others, but has automatically to devise ways to cope with people and to manipulate them with minimum damage to himself."[8] This is how he abandons himself in order to protect himself, but in the process the real self is weakened. When the real self becomes weak the environment becomes more threatening.

A threatening environment evokes in him a dread of others and of self. He becomes hostile and dependent, but tries to repress both because he does not want to give vent to his wrath and annoy others. Repression of hostility has its other repercussions: he feels helpless and defenceless in the hands of a dangerous world. He feels weak, impotent and unlovable. In order to retain his chance of remaining meaningful to himself he adopts self-glorification. The desire is to "lift oneself above others." This he does by adopting interpersonal strategies of defence. These *three* solutions are: his move *towards* people, *away* from people and move *against* people.

The adoption of these defence strategies depends upon individual temperament and his social or familial conditions. A child who moves towards people adopts compliant or self-effacing characteristics. Move against people denotes an aggressive trend: whereas those who move away from others are detached persons. Healthy and neurotic attitude towards others can be demarcated by flexibility or rigidity. A neurotic is not flexible. He is driven by the compulsive nature of his inner necessities. The difference between neurotic drives and healthy strivings "is one between spontaneity and compulsion; between recognizing and denying limitations; between a focus upon the vision of a glorious end-product and a feeling for evolution; between seeming and being, fantasy and truth." (*NHG*, pp.38-39). These three solutions are not mutually exclusive and a person may switch over to other strategies and may develop intra-psychic conflicts.

These inter-personal strategies of defence do not relieve a person of his basic anxiety; "one of the elements involved in basic anxiety" still remains: helplessness in compliant solution, hostility in aggressive solution and isolation in detachment. A person may move from one solution to the other in order to get some sense of wholeness but he will not be able to resolve the conflict. The inner battle continues leading to further confusion and division.

The three neurotic solutions discussed above give us a picture of "types." We must keep in mind that this neat division and classification does not correspond to people in real life or in literary characters. When we speak of human "types" we look at characters from a vantage point of psychological typologies. In life "people tending toward the same main solution" may differ in their human qualities. As Horney puts it:

> To begin with, although people tending toward the same main solution have characteristic similarities they may differ widely with regard to the level of human qualities, gifts or achievements involved. Moreover, what we regard as "types" are actually cross-sections of personalities in which the neurotic process had led to rather extreme developments with pronounced characteristics. But there is always an indeterminate range of intermediate structures deriding any precise classification. These complexities are further enhanced by the fact that, owing to the process of psychic fragmentation, even in extreme instances there

> is often more than one main solution. "Most cases are mixed cases," says Henry James, "and we should not treat our classifications with too much respect." Perhaps it would be more nearly correct to speak of directions of development than of types. (*NHG*, p. 191)

The above qualifications will help us in grasping the complexities of individual characters and appreciating them in their phenomenological realities, rather than identifying neurotic types.

As discussed earlier, a person adopting move towards people is a compliant individual for whom "salvation lies" in love. Under this strategy, there are (i) the self-effacing, and (ii) the morbidly dependent. A self-effacing person *must* not feel superior to others; he must subordinate himself to others in the most appeasing manner; he cultivates qualities of helplessness and martyrdom and expects protection and love in return. He places taboos on all selfishness—wants, needs, desires—as "selfishness." He minimizes them and in the process becomes self-minimizing. It is beyond his purview to be arrogant, conceited or presumptuous. These crippling checks affect his normal human capacity to fight in self-interest. Horney calls it the "shrinking process." He feels secure in his worthlessness. Because it will bring love, approval, acceptance and appreciation. He values his "lovable" qualities and expects that others value him for them. But, when others do not stand upto his expectations, he retaliates. Since he is a self-effacing person, he cannot be violent to others. So, he wallows in self-pity, a sense of guilt and personal inadequacy. His neurotic pride is hurt. Self-hate is generated. His "shoulds" and neurotic claims give rise to tension and he is torn by inner conflicts. In extreme cases, all this may lead to vindictiveness. What form it takes depends upon individual temperament and the damage done.

A morbidly dependent individual is lured by erotic love. For him, it is a "ticket" to paradise. He is also a composite of all lovable qualities. He feels deeply hurt if his qualities are not recognised as he wants them to be; it means total rejection of himself which he cannot tolerate. He fears rejection. He too reacts in a self-destructive way if he is disillusioned. For a morbidly dependent person, it is necessary to love a strong and proud personality, because then he can live vicariously and feel strong in his strength.

On the contrary, an aggressive personality, who follows move against people, wants to master life. He is his very grandiose self. He is assertive, aggressive and self-aggrandized. He wants to overcome all obstacles, master fate, get over all difficulties. But, one cannot call him a strong and healthy personality. It is with compulsive rigidity that he strives to maintain a subjective feeling of superiority. Among the expensive type Horney lists three types: (i) the Narcissistic, (ii) the perfectionists and (iii) the arrogant-vindictive.

The narcissistic wants to master life by "self-admiration and the exercise of charm." (*NHG*, p. 212) The perfectionist seeks to attain the highest prefection and excellence in everything he undertakes, and the arrogant-vindictive has a compulsive need for vindictive triumph. Persons following any one or all these sub-types of expansive drive, are flagrantly disrespectful to anything that speaks of softness, love, compassion or considerateness. They disown all softer feeling as a threat to their whole structure of living. These people do not count on the world to give them anything, probably because their experiences have been bitter in childhood; so they wish to stand by their own visions of life and fight all softness, lest it gives rise to their self-hate.

A detached individual strives for freedom. He places a complete check on his inner and outer demands, and wants neither love nor mastery over life. He lives in an ivory tower, above others and feels proud of his detachment. He resents any intrusion on his well-guarded citadel of privacy and feels consciously superior to others in his self-sufficiency, independence and stoicism. This is, in fact, a flight from responsibilities and is far from the healthv non-attachment eulogised in scriptures.

While inter-personal strategies are working their way to find a defence against basic anxiety, the intra-psychic forces are producing their own problems. A person feels weak because of his alienation from self and the emergent self-hate when his inter-personal demands are not met by others. To minimize the effects of these self-destructive drives, he creates an idealized image of himself. He endows himself with "ulimited powers and with exalted faculties; he becomes a hero, a genius, a supreme lover, a saint, a god." (*NHG*, p. 22) In this he feels happy, posing superior, elevated in his sense of significance. His picture of himself depends upon his strategy. For example, a compliant person valuing love will picture himself as an epitome of all love. This gives him identity. Or for an aggressive individual, his heroism, leadership or strength, give unity and identity. The individual harbouring these imaginary pictures strives to live upto them, all his efforts are directed towards actualising a false image and forsaking the real self.

In his search for glory the neurotic starts making neurotic claims on the world. Whatever grandiose image he has created of himself must be recognised by the world. He cannot realise that he is harbouring an illusion. He lives in the realm of the fantastic. Side by side, his "shoulds" make a claim on him. He "should" be as he has visualised himself to be. There are inner dictates that enumerate his standards for him. All his energies which should take a normal person towards self-actualisation, drag him to actualise the idealised self. The glorified images generate a structure of intra-psychic defence which Horney terms "the pride system."

The "shoulds" and the neurotic claims are difficult to live upto. They stagger in face of realities of life. When they are shattered, the neurotic pride suffers a blow, tension mounts and the neurotic aims at a vindictive revenge to restore it. Depending upon a person's temperament, he may hit harder to get back his imaginary grandeur; he may withdraw, feeling just disinterested; or may try to forget the same by wishing away the incident. Neurotic pride is based on imagined attributes. It is "the climax . . . of the process initiated with the search for glory." (*NHG*, p. 109)

The idealized self-image is made to give a feeling of significance to an individual. It is invested with immense power. But, it is humanly impossible to live upto the standards laid down by the image. When it is not realised, a person feels worthless and develops a despised image. This is his despised self. In the bargain, a neurotic has to counter four selves: the real self, which is already banished; the idealized self which is impossible to attain and is only imaginary; the despised self; and the actual self, which is what he has actualized at the given moment. In a self-actualized person, the distance between real and actual selves is minimum; in a self-alienated individual the gulf is wide.

With the banishment of the real self, alienation takes hold. Self-hate and inner conflicts create a rift in the personality and a war starts within. Horney maintains that the "power and the tenacity of self-hate is astounding." (*NHG*, p. 114) A neurotic may regard himself as a disembodied spirit; he may try to kill his hated self. The onslaughts of self-condemnation, self-accusation and self-hate are difficult to bear. Bonds with reality are severed and deteriorating process starts. There is no spontaneous integration, no ability to give goal direction to life; only a futile and hopeless battle against the world. It is a "pact with the devil" and the result is tragic.

## II

If Horney deals with the process of self-alienation, Abraham Maslow provides us the other side of the picture, that of self-actualization. In simple terms, he considers it "basic gratification plus at least minimum talent, capacity or richness."[9] A person whose basic needs are well-gratified develops into a healthy human being. He is open to the world, more spontaneous in his feelings and responses, is in touch with what he wants, thinks, feels. He trusts his impulses and has a healthy self esteem. His relation to the world is allocentric rather than autocentric. Defining a self-actualized person, Maslow says, he is growth-oriented and is governed by inner determinants. He is "far more autonomous and self-directed." (*TBP*, p. 34)

Maslow's concept of human nature is that of "full humanness." Out of a basic description of full and healthy living emerges the portrait of a mature personality with an objective perception of the self and reality, including acceptance of the personal limitations. The mature person has the ability to give and receive affection, the capacity for creativity and self-fulfilment. A self-actualized person has a sense of responsibility for his actions. He develops a unifying philosophy of life, wanting to live for something, for an objective that signifies life's meaning. Humanness cannot be understood without recognition of values manifest in behaviour, "in the act of valuing, consciousness and behaviour become united."[10] For Stanley Kripper the greatest contribution of humanist psychologists is their theory of values. Maslow suggests that though every day values of man are determined by his culture, the ultimate goal of human beings is the same. This is indeed what Matthew Arnold calls our "best self" which a culture nourishes. It is our truest friend at the time of danger and it unites us in harmony with ourselves. "This is the very self which culture, or the study of perfection, seeks to develop in us; at the expense of our old untransformed self, taking pleasure only in doing what it likes or is used to do, and exposing us to the risk of clashing with every one else who is doing the same !"[11] It is, therefore, essential to find our *best* self and affirm it with all our energy.

Both Horney and Maslow agree that specific social and cultural conditions help in generating neurotic trends. Maslow terms neurosis a deficiency disease and Horney classifies it as a deviation from normal pattern of social behaviour. "Most neurosis involved, along with other complex determinants, ungratified wishes for safety, for belongingness and identification for close relationships and for respect and prestige." (*TPB*, p. 21) Although Third Force psychologists do not deny the role of childhood environment in shaping the neurotic drives of an individual, they lay more stress on the present structure of the psyche and refute the Freudian theory that adult reactions are a repetition of infantile experiences. In *The Neurotic Personality of Our Time* (1987), Karen Horney makes it clear that childhood experiences determine conditions for neuroses but they cannot be considered the only cause of later troubles. Once the child starts feeling "basic anxiety," he seeks for certain defensive strategies to deal with the conditions arising out of his fears and inadequacy. Later, his particular system develops under the influence of external factors, such as familial atmosphere, social and cultural exigencies. His internal necessities to feel whole and the external pressures, mould his adult character.

Social-psychologists emphasise the role of social and cultural forces in shaping man's responses to his surroundings. Erich Fromm affirms that even the most beautiful and the most ugly inclinations of man are not a part of his biologically fixed nature, "but result from the social process which creates man."[12] Man's self-consciousness enables him to contemplate himself as a whole and his interaction with other members of society enable him to bring himself within his own experiential purview; "and thus he can consciously integrate and unify the various aspects of his self, to form a single consistent and coherent and organized personality."[13] It follows then that the basic human nature is common to the entire species of man, only its expression and satisfaction varies according to cultures. His essential inner nature is both weak and strong. It is weak in the sense, it can be easily suppressed or "masked or modified by habits, suggestions, by cultural pressure, by guilt, and so on." (*MP*, p. 129) It is strong as it cannot be fully destroyed. Whether weak or strong, it strives for self-realization.

Its view of human nature as basically growth-oriented makes Third Force psychology especially suitable for the study of literature. Bernard J. Paris, who has been using this methodology for literary, biographical and cultural criticism since 1964, finds it an effective tool for analysing the conflicts and behaviour of literary characters as well as the implied author. He believes that one of the major weaknesses of psychoanalytical study of character has been the interpretation of the present in terms of the past:

> Because of their reliance upon infantile experience to account for the behaviour of the adult, they must often posit events in the character's early life which are not depicted in the text. This results in the generation of crucial explanatory material out of the premises of the theory, with no corroborating literary evidence except the supposed results of the invented experiences, which were inferred from these results to begin with. This procedure has resulted in a justifiable distrust of the psychological study of character.[14]

On the contrary, Horney stresses on the character trends of the adult. It permits us to establish a causal relationship between past and present if there is enough information. But, we can grasp the present structure of the psyche as an inwardly intelligible system. Behaviour can be studied in terms of its function within that system. As a result, we can account for a character's thought, feelings and actions on the basis of what has actually been given.

In the field of literary criticism Third Force psychology is beginning to gain popularity. Works of art are studied in their trans-individual, social settings. Bernard J. Paris's studies in the area demonstrate the applicability of the theories of Maslow and Horney to literary and cultural criticism. *A Psychological Approach to Fiction* presents a scholarly study of important characters: Lord Jim, William Dobbin, Amelia Sedley, Madame de Renal, Maggie Tulliver, Charlie Marlow. Dr. Paris finds these characters a product of the artists's ability to transcend their defences and to see others as they really are, not as he needs to view them. In *Character and Conflict in Jane Austen's Novels* (1978), Dr. Paris applies Horneyan theories to Austen's protagonists and to the implied author. A special number of *The Literary Review* (Vol. XXIV, Winter 1981) contains some erudite articles on Third Force psychology and the study of literature. In his article "Third Force Psychology and the Study of Literature, Biography, Criticism, and Culture," Bernard J. Paris discusses in some detail the phenomena of self-alienation and self-aetualization. He examines the struggle of characters to establish contact with their real self. The healthiest component of literature is not the images of man or its thematic affirmations, but, the allocentric perceptions, in its expressions of Being-love and Being-cognition. Paris also remarks that D.H. Lawrence's psychological concepts are in many ways like those of the Third Force. His "pristine consciousness" is to some extent analogous to the theory of the real self. The principles of Horneyan psychoanalysis enable us to appreciate the author's "genius in mimetic characters." There is a discerning article devoted to Faulkner's Ratliff as an example of self-actualized individual. In another article Patricia R. Eldredge studies the lost self of Charles

Dickens's Esther Summerson. Apart from this special issue, a number of papers published in literary and other scholarly journals examine fictional characters from Horneyan and Maslovian tenets.

A literary artist exposes the inner life of his characters, their relations to each other and the world, embodying his vision of human beings. Third Force psychology gives us a tool to probe the consciousness of these persons, to study their psychic conflicts, to examine their potentiality for full humanness. Man has a future, says Maslow, and it is dynamically active. Only a creative person can manage the future, "only the one who can face novelty with confidence and without fear." (*TPB*, p. 16) An artist, by transcending his autocentricity can see the world in its freshness, and gain an aesthetic perception. Human nature is multiple and there is always a clash between good and evil, the higher and the lower nature. Man aspires for higher values but in his behaviour there still persists "the problem of non-understanding and non-communication."[15] Many theories have been evolved to explain why human behaviour is so erratic and why man cannot lead a happy life. Penfield, a neuro-surgeon discovers that memory is like a tape-recorder. It records all happenings since childhood and keeps it stored. The experiences and feelings locked within, shape our behaviour and reactions in adult life. Social, psychological, biological and cultural forces also have their share in moulding character. Inner struggles and discordant social relations produce neuroses. Emotional stresses, conflicts and frustrations precipitate them. In his explanation of neuroses, Jung utilizes the concept of psychological equilibrium. Neuroses arise out of a clash between an individual's attempt to adjust to some situation and "his constitutional inability to meet the challenge."[16] There are several specific instances in Desai's works where her characters turn neurotic. Psychological researches have shown that psycho-neurotics are generally intelligent people, and Anita Desai's men and women are certainly bright.

Anita Desai conceptualizes the existential problems of her characters; with the help of psycho-analysis we can diagnose them. "Basic anxiety" and "basic needs" are the principal motifs of her works and the main, unfulfilled requirement of her personages. Maya, for example, is always under the pressure of overcoming her insecurity and isolation, by surrendering herself to love. Nirode's needs for love and belonging are not fulfilled resulting in his chaotic mental state. Anita Desai's treatment of the themes of alienation, maladjustment, isolation, the absurdity of human existence, the quest for ultimate meaning, and time as fourth dimension, have an existential leaning. In one of her interviews she admits of having been influenced consciously by Proust, Dostoevsky, Lawrence, Chekhov and Kawabata. We need not work out a parallelism here, but like some of the above writers, her works are also a quest for order and meaning in life. Her protagonists undergo a struggle to find their real self and because of the cramping pressures of anxieties, they lose it. They experience a disparity between the higher needs of the individual inner nature and the unalterable cosmic conditions of existence. Their personal and historical problems play a significant role in exaggerating their existential troubles and in perpetuating their neuroses. Those who are able to comprehend and surmount their personal difficulties, gain a healthy vision of life. Existentialists see human nature as a phenomenon of belief, as an expanding ideal towards aspiration. Even in Sisyphus's efforts to roll the stone uphill again and again, there is hope that the task can be accomplished sooner or later. However, Desai's self-alienated personages are often entangled in personal problems and cannot feel existential *angst*, because they are gripped by neurotic anxiety. Such characters lose their real self, forego human value and create irredeemable conditions for themselves. Others make an effort to establish a contact with the centre and to search the real self.

Like Horney, Anita Desai also believes that childhood experiences determine conditions for neurosis but they are not the only cause of later troubles. Commenting on her solitary and introspective characters's childhood, she observes in her interview with Jasbir Jain:

> I agree that the experiences of childhood are the most vivid and lasting ones. But I'm quite sure that even adult life

> contains many traumatic experiences, for instance fighting in a war may be traumatic experience for a soldier.

She does not fully expose the childhood of her personages but whatever flashbacks are provided are enough to understand them.

Anita Desai's characters tend to forego their vital "self" somewhere during their journey from childhood to adulthood. Any superficial explanation of their behaviour will yield only stereotype personalities, whereas they have much more complex realities behind their inexplicable reactions and rigidities. We meet them, except for Raka in *Fire on the Mountain*, as grown-up individuals, apparently well-settled in life, some of them right into their middle-age, nonetheless disturbed psychologically by forces beyond their comprehension. With the nostalgic flashbacks, Anita Desai reveals their childhood, enabling an analyst to relate the present structure of psyche to their past and to determine the time when they lose their real self. An anonymous letter published in a journal of psychoanalysis points out that a child undergoes traumatic experience if he is made to feel rejected or uncared for. He suffers a psychic death. It is a secret process but it arrests his growth into a wholesome personality. The letter thus sums up the position:

> How is it possible to lose a self ? The treachery, unknown and unthinkable begins with our secret psychic death in childhood—if and when we are not loved and are cut off from our spontaneous wishes. . . . Everything looks normal; no crime was intended; there is no corpse, no guilt. All we can see is the sun rising and setting as usual. But what has happened ? He has been rejected, not only by them, but by himself. . . . What has he lost ? Just one true and vital part of himself: his own yes-feeling, which is his very capacity for growth, his root system.[17]

In sum, these characters have lost touch with their inner reality, the core of their inmost-being in childhood. Their experiences differ in their contents, but all the same they adversely affect their growth as healthy individuals. The refrain adopted by Maya's father is "accept." But without proper training his words lose their effect. Sita struggles to "connect." Nirode "rejects" everything, because childhood images have taught him negation. Bim, Nanda and Raka wish to "forget." All these compulsive drives point back to their severed connection with self.

These characters strive to find a "substitute" for their lost self. Each wants to guard his identity so that he remains meaningful to himself and is able to see himself as someone significant. The imperative urge of each is to "lift himself above others," to guard himself from the hostile and desperate atmosphere perpetuated by a detrimental childhood climate. Maya sees herself as a "doll," to be pampered by all, Monisha glorifies her self-image of an intellectual, superior to other women of Jiban's family. These two characters, ensnared in their delusions of glory, pass through severe alienation and turn self-destructive. In the next chapter we shall analyse their trouble.

## NOTES

1. J.C. Ransom, "Freud and Literature," *The Saturday Review of Literature*, 1 (Oct. 4, 1924), p. 161.
2. Karen Horney, *Neurosis and Human Growth* (1951; rpt. London: Routledge and Kegan Paul, 1965), p. 198. Further references are from this edition and will be indicated in the text by *NHG* and pagination.
3. *A Psychological Approach to Fiction*, p. 24.
4. Third Force Psychologists include Karen Horney, Abraham Maslow, Kurt Goldstein, Otto Rank, C.G. Jung, Erich Fromm, Rollo May, Gordon Allport, Carl Rogers and Ernest Schachtel.
5. Roger Fry, *Vision and Design* (New York: Peter Smith, 1947), p. 14.
6. Erich Fromm, *The Fear of Freedom* (1942; rpt. London: Routledge and Kegan Paul, 1960), p. 25.

7. Abraham Maslow, *Toward a Psychology of Being*, 2nd ed. (New York: D. Van Nostrand, 1968), p. 14. Further references are to this edition and will be cited as *TPB*, along with pagination.
8. Karen Horney, *Our Inner Conflicts* (New York: Norton, 1945), p. 219. Referred to as *OIC*.
9. Abraham Maslow, *Motivation and Personality* (New York: Harper Row, 1956), p. 201. Further references are to this edition and will be indicated in the text by *MP* and pagination.
10. Rollo May, *Psychological and the Human Dilemma* (Princeton: D. Van Nostrand, 1967), p. 220.
11. Matthew Arnold, *Culture and Anarchy*, p. 95.
12. Erich Fromm, *Escape from Freedom* (1941; rpt. New York: Hall, Rinehart and Winson, 1964), p. 12.
13. George Herbert Mead, *On Social Psychology*, ed. Anselm Strauss (1956; rpt. Chicago: University of Chicago Press, 1964), p. 269.
14. Bernard J. Paris, "Third Force Psychology and the Study of Literature, Biography, Criticism and Culture," *The Literary Review*, 24, No. 2 (Winter 1981), pp. 181-221.
15. Thomas A Harris, *I'm O.K. You're O.K.* (New York: Avon Books, 1973), p. 23.
16. James D. Page, *Abnormal Psychology* (1947; rpt. New Delhi: Tata McGraw-Hill, 1970), p. 91.
17. Anonymous, "Finding the Real Self," a letter with a foreword by Karen Horney, *American Journal of Psychoanalysis*, 9 (1949), p. 3.

# 3

# DOWN DARK CORRIDORS

*Cry, the Peacock* (1963) is the tragedy of a father's child. Maya: young, beautiful, intelligent and very sensitive as well as sensuous, fails to grow out of childhood. She is incapable of leading an independent existence. Virtually, whole of her neurotic life is imperceptibly linked with her father's undivided attention. Superficially, it is just a matter of filial affection showered on an only daughter; but, it is more than that and it gathers to itself reverberant contexts of associated cosequences. Her marriage to Gautama only serves to highlight her total involvement with her father. She constantly thinks of him and unconsciously searches him in her husband. Father-daughter love is, in fact, the *leit n otif* of the novel. Critics relate it to Freudian Libido or Lawrentian Oedipus complex and interpret her love as a projection of her "holophilic impulse."[1] For others, her neurosis has existential dimensions, her sickness being almost Kierkegaardian.[2] Some feel that Maya lacks "the virtue of grace and self-possession."[3] However, when we analyse her psychological complexities, we find that there is much more in her character than mere "father fixation" or libidinal instincts.

Maya's character has two very pronounced traits: helplessness, which is almost childlike, and an intense longing for love that is nearly morbid and the root-cause of her trouble. As per Horneyan tenets, she is a compliant person for whom love holds the key to all the problems of life. This defence strategy has two sub-types: the self-effacing and the morbidly dependent. Whereas both value love above everything else in life, it is the morbidly dependent person who finds fulfilment only in a clinging love, it being "the only way to actualise his idealised self." (*NHG*, p. 241) This love makes neurotic claims on others: if he loves the other person so well, he must be loved equally well. Lack of response from the other party is interpreted as rejection.

A serious enquiry into the imperatives of Maya's basic needs to grow into an independent individual will enable us to understand why her attitude becomes one of clinging. The fact that Maya is a motherless child, delicate and sensitive, goes a long way in shaping her tragedy. Her father is a benevolent despot under whose shadow she grows. He focuses all his attention on her, and instead of freedom to grow as an individual, he offers her a life of protection and consequently of submission. A perfectionist himself, he orders his thoughts, his life, learning and career into a set pattern. Maya compares his meticulousness to a "Moghul garden." She remembers fondly how everything with him has grace and dignity. It is

> . . . gracious and exact, where breeding, culture, leisure and comfort have been brought into a nice art, where no single weed is allowed to flower, no single flower to die and remain on the stalk, no single stalk to grow out of its pruned shape. As the streams in a Moghul garden flow musically through channels of carved marble and sandstone, so his thoughts, his life flow, broken into small exquisite patterns by the carving, played upon by altering nuances of light and shade, but never over stepping their limitations, never breaking their bounds, always moving onwards with the same graceful cadence. (*CP*, p. 45)

Maya is brought up into this orderly world of the father. She discerns, with the acute insight natural to a child, that he has special affection for her. She reminisces during one of her nostalgic moments, "I had been a wayward and high-strung child." Later, in her married life, whenever she is upset, her ardent wish is to run to her father for assurance, and hear those "mesmerising words . . . in his deep tones." (*CP*, p. 52) In her childhood, he used to take her in his arms, wipe her tears and pacify her, irrespective of the gravity or triviality of her fears. Maya grows up physically, but he does not give her a chance to get out of this childhood stage. Old words are replaced by new, more appropriate, terms, "the charm was expanded, new phrases were enveloped to give me more room for thought." (*CP*, p. 52) Maya cannot arrive at a correct self-evaluation. Father's over-protective and sickly love, dealt out to her with unconcealed partiality, does not allow her any independence to think and grow as an entity.

Maya's prominent wish is never to displease her father. She is scared of losing his affection because on it rests her security and sense of belonging. She has seen the fate of her rebel-brother Arjuna. He has lost father's affection by wriggling out the perfectionist regime. Father's tight-lipped coldness towards him is too ill-concealed to escape Maya's notice. She recollects that father was terse, cold and grim with Arjuna, "with me he never was, no matter what I did—even I noted the difference, and felt uncomfortable." (*CP*, p. 133) Two forces work on Maya's psyche—the strict and orderly world of father and his blind adoration; she cannot disregard either.

Since pleasing father is of paramount importance to Maya, it becomes her primary concern and subsequently, her basic anxiety. In order to remain his adored and admired child she leans more and more on him and later, on Gautama; losing her real self in the bargain. Karen Horney categorically refers to these "injurious influences" which prevent a child from arriving at correct self-evaluation. She elaborates:

> A blind adoration may inflate his feeling of significance. He may feel wanted and appreciated not for what he is but merely for satisfying his parent's needs for adoration, and prestige and power. A rigid regime of perfectionist standards may evoke in him a feeling of inferiority for not measuring

> up to such demands. . . . Moves towards autonomy or independence may be ridiculed. (*NHG*, p. 87)

Father's love hampers her growth "from acorn into oak tree." (*NHG*, p. 18) In fact, the love Maya gets is a projection of father's own inadequacy, the expression of a neurotic urge to possess the child. Jasbir Jain also feels that her father could give Maya attention and protection but not real love. Whatever he could give her as a semblance of love was a "manifestation of power" and the "relationship fed on his own ego. Maya is the sacrifice offered at the altar of his own image."[4] Consequently, Maya's basic needs for love and belongingness are not gratified in the real sense. Healthy development of her personality is blocked. She remains a "light-headed child" all through her life.

Maya's childhood world of fantasies and adult world of realities clash, producing more imbalances in her life. She wants to perpetuate the "fairy-tale" atmosphere; at the same time, she is aware of the demands of a grown-up, mature world of a married woman. She has an urge to grapple with the realities of life, to understand her in-laws, to charm Gautama, not with child-like demands but by her feminine charm. There are moments when she sincerely tries to follow Gautama's philosophy of the *Gita*. Unfortunately, however, these urges to experience the realities of life are too feeble to last longer. The child in her takes over and she once more treads on familiar grounds.

Since the novel opens with the death of her pet dog, Toto, we have a glimpse of her irreparably shaken sensitivity. Maya is shattered by a reality too hard to bear. Her imagination takes full charge of her reasoning. She sees death lurking somewhere nearby. Death of Toto evokes a faint fear; her "tear-hazed vision" is blurred by a horrifying sense of doom. She records the presence of a shadowy something, "that prodded me into admitting that it was not my pet's death alone that I mourned today, but another sorrow, unremembered, perhaps as yet not even experienced, and filled me with this despair." (*CP*, p. 8) To alleviate her suffering, she needs the assuring warmth of Gautama's company, as she would have needed and certainly received from her father.

Maya's tendency to depend on her father and then on her husband in a clinging relationship is in response to the demands of her psyche to guard against the onslaught of a hostile world. She has lost the ability to master her life and constantly needs a psychological prop. This is perhaps the reason why she agrees to marry a man much older to herself. She can lean on him and feel secure. Gautama's irritated exhortations, "you have a very obvious father-obsession," (*CP*, p. 146) is neither incorrect nor misplaced in the sense that for Maya, father is the most important and the strongest motivating force in life. However, Gautama's further remark regarding her Freudian fixation is miscalculated. In Horneyan sense, it is not libidinal instinct, it is simply her search for glory.

All through her life Maya has seen herself from her father's eyes: his "treasure" to be protected. Now, as a grown-up woman she cannot relate herself to the realities of married life. Inner demands and outer liabilities create a conflicting situation. In Gautama's family the atmosphere is heavily charged with intellectual, social and political discussions. Here, "one did not speak of love, far less of affection." (*CP*, p. 46) Maya cannot participate in their ceaseless and heated debates. She feels inferior. She is left out of it "with a naturalness I had to accept for they knew I would not understand a matter so involved, and I knew it myself." (*CP*, pp. 48-49) With her they discuss babies, shopping, meals and marriages, for "I was their toy, their indulgence, not to be taken seriously, and the world I came from was less than that—it was a luxury they considered it a crime to suffer, and so damned it with dismissal." (*CP*, p. 42) Maya, therefore, tries to find some solution to recover her dwindling sense of significance. When man feels inferior in society his strongest desire is to raise himself above others.

> If he had a sense of belonging, his feeling inferior to others would not be so serious a handicap. But living in a competitive society, and feeling at bottom—as it were—isolated and hostile, he can develop an urgent need *to lift him above others*. (*NHG*, p. 21)

Maya cannot, by temperament and training, be one with her in-laws. To give her life a meaning and to save herself from self-hate she holds on to her identity.

Identity, for Maya, rests in keeping intact her childhood. This she achieves by re-creating her fairy-tale world of Arabian Nights and "lovely English and Irish fairy tales . . . in which much was excluded, which grew steadily more restricted, unnatural even, and in which I lived as a toy princess in a toy world." (*CP*, p. 89) Maya realises the unreality of her situation but she cannot come out of it. There is no genuine attempt at self-analysis. Jasbir Jain remarks that Maya's unhappiness is an outcome of her own consciousness and it is in part related to the process of her growing up.[5] Gautama is irritated at her temper tantrums: " Neurotic . . . Neurotic, that is what you are. A spoilt baby, so spoilt she can't bear one adverse word. Everyone must bring a present for little Maya—that is what her father has taught her." (*CP*, p. 115) The devitalising love received in childhood separate her consciousness from physical reality around and within her, which finally destabilises her real self.

In order to establish her uniqueness and self-importance, Maya builds around herself a bower of bougainvillaea and jasmine buds "palpitating with living breath, open, white, virginal." (*CP*, p. 106) Anyone who does not fit into it is inferior—Gautama, his family, his relatives are all lesser mortals, lacking in finer sensitivities. She is desperate when Gautama cannot distinguish between the fragrance of Petunias and lime-blossoms. She alienates herself from Leila and Pom just because they accept life as it is. Mrs. Lal and other women at the party do not measure up to her expectations, as such she reacts violently. The sight of prostitutes horrifies her because they do not see the *truth* in living. They are engrossed in the "gross and *useless*" they "don't see what really matters. All the *truth* in living just passes them by, and I am so sorry for anyone . . . who misses it." (*CP*, p. 91) She reiterates that she is different from them all. Her uniqueness signifies her separate identity.

This separate identity does not give her sufficient sense of security. Her real self is pushed in the background. Move towards false self does not promise healthy mental state. Such subtleties and perversities of feeling are finely explored in the case of Monisha and Nirode in *Voices in the City*, where the frustrating strains of unconscious life disintegrate the characters. Nanda Kaul in *Fire on the Mountain* recasts her childhood fantasies not only to hold the interest of her great grand-daughter but also to give herself the much-needed feeling of significance. The role of self-importance in human life is substantiated by Ravi in "Games at Twilight." Forgotten by his game-mates, he feels humiliated. In his search for glory, he refuses to participate in their games and is "silenced by a terrible sense of his insignificance." (*GAT*, p. 10) Here it may appear to be a temporary mood tantrum of a child, but his sulkiness suggests that Mrs. Desai's characters are sensitive to failure and neglect. They often struggle to achieve triumph—to it through unhealthy drives like neurotic compulsions or healthy epiphany.

Maya's sense of triumph and self-importance is closely allied to her search for glory. It is a compulsive drive and does not allow her awareness and understanding of herself. Hers is a dissociated personality, as such she suffers a dichotomy of her two selves—real and pseudo. Some critics believe that Anita Desai paints unyielding personages who look back to "protect their vision of the secret world of passion and beauty."[6] Sometimes, this insight provides value leading to acceptance of actuality. However, in certain cases the tendency to look back only denotes a character's search for glory, as in Maya's case. Freud calls it "regression." D.H. Lawrence also maintains that when the enclosure of the ego is final and when men live a hermetically sealed life, insulated from all experience, they lose the sense of harmony within and without. Philosophically speaking, unhappiness springs up because although each man lives in an apparent relationship with family, friends and society, he lives in self-isolation. J. Krishnamurthy elaborates it as living with an "image." Each individual makes his own image of himself and of others. He loves these images, thus failing to establish real relationship. Man cannot break away from the past. "We *are* the past and there is no freedom in the past. So, that is our life, a constant battle, the past, modified by the present, moving into the future—which is still the movement of the past though modified."[7] Man clings to the image in order to get a sense of security and escape the confusion created by this unreal relationship. This entails no real freedom for the self to grow. In Horneyan language, making a self-image, investing it with fantastic powers, idealizing it and then living it, tantamounts to the Faustian "devil's pact." The price is to be paid in the form of neurotic troubles that arise and "pave the way to an inner hell of self-contempt and self-torment. By taking this road, the individual is in fact losing his soul—his real self." (*NHG*, p. 39) Maslow gives us another side of the same picture and observes that when our exemplary self-image which makes over-perfect demands on ourselves, "breaks down under insight,"[8] can we see perfection and beauty of full humanness. Unfortunately, Maya's vision of beauty and harmony is distorted because hers is a dissociated consciousness, unable to liberate the forces of spontaneous growth.

Considering her timidity, child-like dependence and her inability to master her life, Maya would be lost without the protection of love around her. So far it was father's protective embrace. She was secure in it. The flow of love, admiration and sympathy is suddenly interrupted when Gautama shows an aversion to too much physical contact. She feels neglected, rejected and unwanted. Describing the importance of love for a self-effacing person Horney emphatically maintains that this type cannot stand being alone. At such moments they are tortured by self-accusation and are stricken by an unnamed terror. Maya is frightened to be without company because she has no rapprochment with the real self. As long as Gautama attends to her, she feels grateful and is flooded with "tenderness and gratitude." She thinks of him as her protector and guardian. A slight touch of his fingers brings out spontaneous reaction of joy: "Fall, fall, long fall into the soft velvet well of the primordium, of original instinct, of first-formed love." (*CP*, p. 11) When he does not respond in the expected manner, her neurotic pride is hurt; she feels the insult of rejection.

In Part II of the novel, Maya complains of Gautama's callousness. He is unconcerned about her misery, her physical and psychological demands:

> Giving me an opal ring to wear on my finger, he did not notice the translucent skin beneath, the blue flashing veins

> that ran under and out of the bridge of gold and jolted me into smiling with pleasure each time I saw it . . . he did not give another thought to me, to either the soft, willing body or the lonely, wanting mind that waited near his bed. (*CP*, p. 9)

This is not a commonplace household situation showing a wife grumbling against an over-busy husband. It is the cry of an agonised woman feeling lonely and unwanted. Maya suffers acutely. She clings more and more to him, intrigued by his arrogance. She must keep herself intact despite the ever-widening inner division. She can achieve this if she merges herself with him. Unconsciously, she surrenders to him.

The wish to surrender to a stronger personality is inherent in a morbidly dependent character. Maya is, apparently, a composite of all lovable qualities. She is helpless, suffering, humble, loving, and hence lovable. Her expansive traits remain suppressed in her unconscious, because she does not want to master her life. Before marriage father was there on whom she externalised, and felt strong in his strength; now, there is Gautama. He is superior to her in many ways—age, arrogance, knowledge and in his capacity to rule over her. For Maya, both father and husband are "magic helpers"[9] to protect her from a feeling of inadequacy. Erich Fromm uses this term to represent the outside power on whom a helpless or a dependent person projects all his longings, and develops a symbolic relationship. That Maya has always admired him for his superiority, is clear when she decides not to admire him for "this superior plane he always managed to elevate himself onto when I tried to involve him in my matters, my wants and cares. . . ." (*CP*, p. 113) Through him she obtains the supreme confirmation of her "self."

Maya's persistent demands for "contact, relationship, communion" cannot be termed as "oral erotic." For her it simply means a flight from "the embrace of protection to embrace of love." (*CP*, p. 95) There are moments when she shows an almost aggressive urge for sexual union with Gautama. But, asleep or awake, Gautama is a far-off figure, who cannot be one with her in her world of senses. She expresses her sadness with the help of the imagery of withered flowers. The lifeless roses and carnations on her dressing table "belonging to yesterday, corpses of today," are very much like her desires.

Anita Desai establishes an identity between setting and the mental state of Maya, in order to show her desires for love and her dread of death. That Maya wants a sexual union is clearly perceptible in her contemplation and exultation on seeing the male and female papaya trees in the garden. The description is richly erotic:

> . . . I contemplated that, smiling with pleasure at the thought of those long streamers of bridal flowers that flow out of the core of the female papaya tree and twine about her slim trunk, and the firm, wax-petalled blossoms that leap directly out of the solid trunk of the male. . . . Besides, if I could pleasure in contemplation of the male papaya, how much more food for delight in this male companion, surely. (*CP*, p. 92)

Her longing to drown herself in love is further enriched and intensified by the vibrating insect imagery in the novel.

While Maya craves for love, Gautama flees it. His unconcerned and detached attitude is as much puzzling to the readers as it is to Maya. He has a strong tendency to recoil from touch or physical nearness. Some critics assign it to their temperamental incompatibility—she being hyper-sensitive and he being taciturn. A close examination, however, indicates deep psychological reasons. By any standard Gautama is not a neurotic character. He is a normal human being, leading a sufficiently healthy life. His outlook has been formed by the "self-sacrificing years of study and hard work, his refusal to concede, to compromise. . . . " (*CP*, p. 93) The events of his early life—his freedom-fighter father always on the move, mother left to manage things—give him a sense of responsibility. He is resigned and reserved by nature. This attitude could change into neurotic compulsions but Gautama feeds it with the philosophy of the *Gita* and tries hard to turn it into a healthy striving for detachment. But, his error lies in his rigidity. He is unable to fuse his "ought" and "is." He wants to change

Maya as he thinks she "ought" to be, instead of understanding her as she actually "is."

Gautama shrinks from contact because he is afraid of emotions. In order to hide his fear, he becomes sarcastic, passive or disinterested. When one probes deeper into these moves, one comprehends his dislike of himself. Gautama becomes aware of his weakness in face of Maya's superiority at emotional level. In moments of irritation, he vomits all his spite, casting derogatory remarks not only on her but on her father too. Maya cannot understand the intricacies of his psyche. Their trouble acquires a deeper tinge as there is no possibility of any fruitful solution. They live in separate worlds and "did not even agree on which points, on what grounds this closeness of mind was necessary." (*CP*, p. 19) Like Dostoevsky's underground man, Gautama seems to say, "For a woman, all resurrection, all salvation, from whatever perdition lies in love; in fact, it is her only way to it."[10]

The psychology of characters, the events and the setting in *Cry, the Peacock* coalesce with the imagery radiating through the narrative. The novelist highlights Maya's sexual demands with the help of two powerful symbols: the peacock's voluptuous dance and the mating calls of pigeons. The title of the novel also symbolises the agony of an unfulfilled desire. The cries of the dancing peacocks "*pia, pia, Mio, Mio,*" assimilate in Maya's mind with her own anguish. She weeps for them as well as for herself, "knowing their words to be mine." (*CP*, p. 97) The cooing of pigeons in her verandah evoke in her "a longing, a dread, a search for solution, a despair." (*CP*, p. 35)

Unfortunately, what Maya thinks of as love is not love in the true sense of the word. It is a means to relieve her anxiety. It has no motivating force and is symptomatic of her insecurities. Love signifies full faith. It is a commitment without any guarantee; it means a readiness to give oneself up completely. Maya cannot commit herself to others selflessly because she lacks faith in herself. Fromm observes that in such cases "while one is consciously afraid of not being loved, the real, though unconscious, fear is that of loving. To love means to commit oneself without guarantee."[11] Since faith in others entails an awareness of the existence of the "self," conviction of one's identity is an essential factor. Maya is the prisoner of her own defence mechanism where safety and security are of primary importance. Love, as she sees it, not as it really means, is the only answer. She chides Gautama, "You know nothing of me—and of how I can love. How I *want* to love. How it is *important* to me." (*CP*, p. 112) Here is a love that says, "I love you because I need you." Erich Fromm terms it "immature" love. It does not give the sense of sharing and of oneness; rather it produces a feeling of dependence.

Perfect and ideal love, as Maya visualises, belongs to the realm of the fantastic. Gautama is clear about it. He points out that love cannot remain an ideal in real life. Ultimately, it boils down to paying bills, rearing children and worrying for them. He agrees that "it is rather shocking to reduce one's ideals to mundane superfluities, and equally shocking to realise that these superfluities are the ideals themselves." (*CP*, p. 21) But, that is the reality of existence and has to be faced. On the contrary, Maya conceives of love as an ecstatic feeling, perhaps as depicted on Keats's Grecian urn. When it is not fulfilled, she is enfeebled by her self-alienating forces within; she cannot integrate the power of her vital self. Fear of death preoccupies her.

Throughout the novel, we are given to feel that the albino priest's predictions and Gautama's lack of sympathetic understanding are the fountain-heads of Maya's neurosis. Maya also lays the blame on Gautama who is calm and detached as "the meditator beneath the *sal* tree," (*CP*, p. 8) and on the priest who remains near her consciousness always, either as a magician or as an Evil-power. Being weak-willed and an epitome of helplessness, as her strategy requires her to be, she has, in fact, developed the habit of blaming others for her calamities. Not for a moment it occurs to her that she has created the mental hell for herself, others have just accelerated it. Had she displayed some will-power, she would have mastered the situation. External chances are available—Gautama's therapeutic philosophy of the *Gita*, Leila's example of facing all the vicissitudes of life, Arjuna's rebellious "growing out of crib." But, her father's fatalism has a stronger hold on her. There is no illumination, no knowledge, only objectification.

When the outside world cannot help her, she looks within, but unfortunately the centre within is the false centre, the glorified self, not the real core of Being. Gautama counsels her to look at the world from a detached angle otherwise "life will remain an emptiness to you and you will continue to reach out and grasp for everything—every desirable thing in view, and imagine you have filled your life and given meaning to your existence by doing so." (*CP*, p. 116) Gautama's words are meaningful, but Maya has already eliminated the real inner world of personal experience, in order to satisfy her idealised self. Consequently, she has lost hold on feelings.

It is true that Maya's difficulties start with the albino priest's prediction because his words shatter her self-image. Neither Gautama's logic, nor father's fatalistic exhortations to "accept" could help her to get over the anxiety. The fact remains that Maya has an exaggerated opinion of herself which falsifies reality. Unawares, she has fabricated a "fairy tale" realm, away from all pain. She is a denizen of this toy world, where even breakfast was "as good as a revel of elves and fairies who feast on melons and syrups by moonlight." (*CP*, p. 43) In this world she is not one of those ordinary mortals who can be wiped away by fate. She has perfected her image as a being "different" from others. She resents the idea that one "has to put up with mediocrity" in everyday life. Her refrain is "I am different from all of you." Naturally, fate should give her preferential treatment.

Horney says that neurotics make secret claim toward life and want that their life should be as they visualise it. They cannot face facts. It is because their claims clamour, "because I am something extra special, I am entitled to" be treated "in accord with his grandiose notions about himself." (*NHG*, p.41) This includes demands made on fate also. Maya demands preferential treatment from all. The realisation that fate is relentless, and it will strike her comes to her as a blow. She cannot escape the pains and sufferings of a hard, harsh, protean reality. Somewhere in her unconscious her impotence and finitude gnaw at her. After all, she is not a wood-nymph or a fairy living in a protected atmosphere of divine bliss and beauty. It means she is ordinary. To live the life of an ordinary human, is beyond the scope of her neurotic claims. In these circumstances, the only significant thing is to cling to life. To come back to everyday world means to return to knowledge. Maya dreads knowledge as a dark pit "stark, hard and ultimate as the rock-bottom of a dry well." (*CP*, p. 186)

As a result of this, she reacts violently to anything that is real, definite and concrete. Time is definite—she abhors it. "Only now" is of vital importance. Tomorrow is "closely linked to the chain of time," as such she avoids thinking of it. Time means an "inevitable order of attachment, its disintegration, and then, the deluge." (*CP*, p. 10) Deluge here signifies death, a finality she would fain escape. Illusion is the safest refuge. And being *Maya* (delusion) herself, she is capable of nothing but "illusions, imagining them to be real."

With her real centre not at her command, Maya is torn by strange turmoil within and without. Her inner dictates come out with many exhortations: she should not be involved, she should accept life, she should practise non-attachment. This is the "tyranny of her shoulds," which, along with her neurotic claims on the outside world, generate severe inner conflicts. Frantically, she looks for security in the path Gautama suggests. But, being an inhabitant of a world of heightened sensitivity, it offers her no safety. His world, "however safe, was so very drab and no longer offered me security." (*CP*, p. 198) She fails to find an anchorage in Gautama's philosophy. Problems multiply when her neurotic claims make unreasonable demands on others. That all must attend to her, shows her egocentricity. She is disillusioned in her friends and wails that she has no friend and "whomsoever I turned for reassurance, betrayed me now." (*CP*, p. 64) Self-pity grips her and she chafes bitterly that the world is no more "like a toy specially made for me, painted in my favourite colours, set moving to my favourite tunes." (*CP*, p. 36) Failure on all these fronts generates fear, because failure means defeat and its reaction is the anger of frustration.

As a morbidly dependent person, Maya cannot express her rage openly. That would not be commensurate with her self-image of a loving and selfless individual. So, she hides her aggressive traits behind her self-effacing and self-minimizing processes. She projects herself as a helpless, suffering martyr; a childless woman, gripped by the misfortune of her pet's death. Her act of pillow-beating and crying piteously is what Horney terms the "shrinking process" wherein she sees herself as a helpless child. These initial expressions lead to self-pity. Psychosomatic symptoms, like slitting headaches and fever, followed by delirium, occur. Maya becomes vindictive when finally the self alienates itself from the real centre; and self-hate takes hold.

Self-hate is the logical outcome of a conflict between Maya's pride system and her real self. It is a war between the healthy and neurotic forces, i.e. between constructive and destructive elements. Karen Horney calls it "the central inner conflict." (*NHG*, p. 112) Anita Desai presents Maya's tussle using mirror imagery. As she gazes in the mirror, she sees her own body detach itself from her soul and "float away, to rest upon the dim mirror where I could gaze upon it from a cool distance." (*CP*, p. 105) This detached body is her glorified self and the thing it is severed from is the actual self. Maya studies her reflection in the mirror. It is:

> ... the round, childish face, pretty, plump and pampered, its smooth, silken skin with one, small velvet mole; the small, shell-like ears curling round petty ignorance; the soft, overful lips arched with the vulnerable sweetness; the long, curled lashes and the very heavy, very dark black brows; the silly collection of curls, a flower pinned to them—a pink flower, a child's choice of a posy. (*CP*, p. 105)

This lovable child is the glorified self of Maya. She hates it because she is aware that the child's face cannot captivate Gautama. Her words are meaningful: "I gazed long at each feature of the image before me, so like a painting on a chocolate box, and hated it fiercely. Hate was a new emotion to me, and, in trespassing upon it, I entered a new vista of knowledge." (*CP*, pp. 105-6) At another place, mirror is the "mercurial cage." She strikes at it in order to get rid of an "absurd" reflection. This is the first glimpse of her acute self-hate turning into self-destructive tendencies. The mirror comes down crashing; their faces look grotesque, and Maya, pressing her face to the glass bursts out laughing. Her weird action suggests total loss of control.

Virginia Woolf employs mirror imagery to suggest the presence of the self in the reflection. In *Mrs. Dalloway*, when Clarissa looks at her image in the mirror, she sees Septimus standing behind it. Since Septimus is intended to be the double of Clarissa, his presence is her "self," complementary to her. As Virginia Woolf remarks, her intention was to present "the world seen by the sane and the insane side by side."[12] Working out an analogy here, we see the two selves of Maya in conflict: the actual self hating the glorified self. In Conrad's *The Secret Sharer* also, the secret self merges with the mirrored self. Maya's real self is banished. She is estranged from herself and depersonalization takes place.

As a result of depersonalization, Maya feels, many a time, that she is not human, only a dream: "Maya—my very name means nothing, is nothing but an illusion." (*CP*, p. 172) From "nothingness" she turns into a "caged monkey." This indicates loss of identity. In *The Waves*, Rhoda describes her precarious moments of near-madness in terms of lost identity: "I came to the puddle. I could not cross it. Identity failed me. We are nothing, I said and fell."[13] When the inner self loses the "self-world" relationship, disorientation takes place. Maya's subjective and objective awareness is blurred. She loses interest in the things outside herself. This is a dangerous state when a person goes into psychotic condition, which in common parlance we know as insanity or madness. Maya's condition deteriorates rapidly. Within months she crosses the borderline into insanity.

A clear picture of Maya's psyche is provided in terms of various motifs, dreams and hallucinations running through the narrative. A recurrent image is that of the moon. To suggest the fast deteriorating mental state of Maya, Anita Desai uses moon symbolism according to the subjectivity of the heroine. In her acutely disturbed state, the moon appears to her as sinister and ghastly, "a demoniac creature, the fierce dancer... accompanied by a deafening roar of silent drums." (*CP*, p. 28)

Indeed, it becomes one with Kathakali dancer and frightens Maya. Later, it is depicted as a full-bosomed woman glowing across the sky. Here, the novelist acknowledges the mystery and uniqueness of psyche of which it is the ruling planet. Then the moon appears like:

> . . . a great multifoliate rose, waxen white, virginal, chaste and absolutely white, casting a light that was holy in its purity, a soft suffusing glow of its chastity, casting its reflection upon the night with a vast, tender mother love. (*CP*, p. 208)

Gautama comes between Maya and her worshipped moon, as such she chooses to punish him. Symbolically, the position of the moon in the sky parallels the lucidity of the thoughts of Maya, which progress in the same degree and the moon becomes a symbol of her psyche.

Other recurring symbols in the novel are those of reptiles—snakes, iguanas and lizards. Maya's terror of an imaginary snake can be interpreted as the fear of the *Maya* (delusion) of the Hindu philosophy, that coils round us. It is in the collective unconscious of the Hindus. Psychologically, reptiles stand for sexual urge. But, this fear, here, is indicative of her morbidity and fast deteriorating psychic condition. Under high fever, the dancer, the priest, rats, snakes, all become one, including her father. The forces within her react to the deteriorating process. Horney states that the danger of the self-destructive drive appears in the form of "succinct symbols, such as a homicidal maniac, Dracula, monster, a white whale or ghosts." (*NHG*, p. 3) This fear is the nucleus of many unknown fears. In Maya, the ingrained fear of death—a mysterious force—is at the bottom of her weird dreams. We are reminded of Arun Joshi's hero, Som Bhaskar, in *The Last Labyrinth*,[14] haunted by death neurosis.

Psychologists agree that it is impossible to live with such horror. A person needs to assuage it. Maya externalises her trouble. She projects her self-hate on Gautama. Her primary instinct is self-preservation. She convinces herself that Gautama does not love life. Moreover, he has hurt her neurotic pride by rejecting her love. In order to subdue her inner turmoil, she kills him in a vindictive rage.

In sum, the key to understanding Maya's character lies in comprehending her divided self. There is no attempt on her part at self-analysis to apprehend her demands. The fast withering self and the receding contact with outer world, leave the core of her integrity impaired. Her failure to find life and more of it, becomes an appalling crime. She condemns Gautama to death for it and then, burdened with guilt, and haunted by self-contempt, self-accusation and self-hate, she drags herself into complete darkness of the world of the insane.

## II

Monisha's presence in *Voices in the City* (1965), and her ultimate act of violence—suicide—have been questioned by many critics. Regarding her persence, it is felt that she is a side-character and hence not worthy of much attention, the focus being on Nirode and Calcutta city. That is why, perhaps, the author left her as an "unconvincing" character. According to B. Ramchandra Rao, "she is very vaguely drawn and flits like a ghost in the consciousness of her brother and her younger sister."[15] Her suicide, a critic feels, is virtually "a confession of failure" on the part of the author. For others, she is only a "variation of Maya" in her loneliness and sensitivity. As these scholars focus only on Nirode and his crises against the back-drop of Calcutta, they find Monisha too melodramatic and just unnecessary. Jasbir Jain recognises Monisha's struggle to achieve wholeness but views her suicide and rebellion as an act of rejection. However, I shall analyse here Monisha's conflicts to suggest that she is a distinct personality in her own right.

A will-less, helpless and passive woman, Monisha stands in direct contrast to Maya. If Maya's trouble lies, as we have seen, in her rich sensuality, Monisha's difficulties arise due to her passivity. Anita Desai uses the narrative technique of diary in order to record Monisha's psychic turmoil. Married into a placid, middle-class family, and to a prosaically dull husband, she is unable to adjust to her environment. She stoically refuses to identify herself with her in-laws's family. She is charged of theft and commits suicide. Monisha suppresses her emotions and makes no attempt whatsoever to analyse herself. Instead, she yearns for greater will-lessness, which is symptomatic of severe neurosis. From Horneyan psycho-analytical angle, Monisha adopts the strategy of resignation.

A person following the strategy of withdrawal has a strong tendency to remove himself from the "inner battlefield" in order to relieve his tensions. He does not participate in the act of living and becomes an onlooker on life. He lacks aspirations, efforts and the will for achievement. By stifling his wishes, he erroneously feels satisfied at having reached a state of non-attachment, happy that he has no expectations from life and from others. He shows a fear for emotional involvement, because it may curtail his freedom. Thus, by withdrawing himself from his surroundings into a world of his own, he wants to save his individuality, but unfortunately, as this withdrawal is not a healthy man's detachment, it leads to disintegration. His main aim—to keep himself intact—is defeated in itself. He is alienated from himself. He forgets that an individual "cannot grow in a vacuum, without closeness to and friction with other human beings." (*NHG*, p. 276)

Monisha's character revolves around two main constituents: the silence and a "touch of malice" inherited from her father, and a morbid temperament, hinted at by aunt Lila. Parental indifference and familial disorder characterize her childhood. The three siblings of Monisha respond differently to the environment according to their temperament. The remoteness of home puzzles her. There is an element of unknown in the atmosphere. As a result she withdraws into a world of her own, remains aloof and retains it in her relationship later. Her incapacity to relate herself to her family creates "basic anxiety." She glorifies herself as a lonely and cold person—almost stoic—different from the mass of women she sees around her. The refrain "I am different from them all," reverberating through *Cry, the Peacock* also echoes throughout Monisha's diary. It spells disaster for both. In fact, feeling "different" from others and being a non-conformist is a difficult proposition in itself. If one has achieved an exalted state of transcending one's own individual life and find atonement, one may get happiness in this state, but an ordinary person is confronted with the problem of "separateness" if he clings to the illusion of being unique in himself. Anita Desai is interested in characters who are not average and have the courage to choose untrodden paths. Harish, for example, in her short story "Surface Texture," has the boldness to give up his job and a secure life, and wander in search of interesting surfaces. However, only those who, like Harish, have a tendency towards autonomy can gain self-sufficiency and strength by such denials of the ordinary ways of life. Those who forsake their self and merge in the non-self, giving up will, freedom, self-sufficiency, self-control and autonomy, suffer self-alienation. This quest for the "self" bears fruit only when one is able to establish a "communication with the outer world to improve along with improvement in the development of the personality, along with its integration and wholeness, and along with freedom from civil war among the various portions of the personality, i e. perception of reality should improve. (*FRHN*, pp. 161-62) Maya's violent reaction to the ordinariness of the people at Lal's party and Monisha's sarcastic reflections on the women "who follow five paces behind their men," spending their lives "waiting for nothing," (*VC*, p. 220) speak not only of Maya and Monisha's misplaced urge to stay distinct from the ordinary people, but also indicate their relentless quest to elevate their "self" by posing superior to others.

Between her mother's epicurean temperament and father's stoicity, Monisha prefers the latter, because her father is a suffering martyr. Glorification of his traits in herself give her heroic dimensions. Her aloofness becomes her wisdom; her passivity acquires the colour of an independent personality. "I am too silent for them I know: they all distrust silence," Monisha observes. She satisfies all her inner needs by substituting self-idealization for the pain of inferiority and anxiety. Monisha feels elevated in her silence because Jiban's family abhors it. It helps her to be on an imperious plane. There are scattered references to it throughout her diary, "My silence, I find, has powers over others." (*VC*, p. 130) Jiban recognizes her unfriendly behaviour and exhorts, " 'Be a little friendly to them,' Jiban begs, 'That is all they ask of you—a little friendliness.' " (*VC*, p. 118)

During girlhood, her parents interpret her silence and aloofness as an inclination towards "morbidity." As a precautionary measure to curb her unhealthy tendencies, they force her into a marriage with a man unsuitable to her taste and temperament, thinking that, "it would be a good thing for her to be settled into such a stolid, unimaginative family as that, just sufficiently educated to accept her with tolerance." (*VC*, p. 199) Socially, the joint family, with so many traditional bindings, is impossible to live with. Even Nikhil, Monisha's nephew, is exasperated by this "bad system" as he terms it; it is so detrimental to individual growth and freedom. But, psychologically, it is more of a shattering experience for Monisha than it socially is. She gets the first blow at the reception, "arranged by the heads of this many-headed family." (*VC*, p. 109) She is made to touch the feet of a large number of aunts and uncles. Later on, life is reduced to cooking and washing which hurts her pride further. "To sort the husk from the rice, to wash and iron and to talk and sleep, when this is not what one believes in. . . ." (*VC*, p. 121) What she wants is to "live the clean, husked, irreducible life."

Some critics ascribe her unhappiness to her existential quest for meaning in life, and her ultimate frustration at not finding anything to sustain her. It is, nevertheless, arguable that Monisha's trouble is more of the nature of personal problems than existential. She cannot get over her neurotic despair. It is incorrect to judge the magnitude of her troubles by the intensity of her feelings. In fact, all her efforts are directed towards alleviating her personal crisis. Existential problems, on the other hand, arise out of a disparity between man's natural wants for life, choice and freedom, and the unchangeable cosmic conditions of existence. They are irremediable and common to all humanity. Monisha does not suffer existential *angst* but only neurotic anxiety.

Meena Shirwadkar[16] assigns Monisha's sufferings to her childless state. It is true that traditional Indian society looks down upon a childless woman. A woman gains status only as a mother. But, in Monisha's case, the awareness of her low profile in family and in society is punched so unceremoniously daily into her that it becomes one of the reasons for her inferiority complex. Every time she hears them talk of "blocked tubes," the urge on her part is to look down upon them from a superior height of her silent defiance.

All the female members of her husband's family, as also other Bengali women, traditional and patient, are the target of her contempt. She broods over their lot, "waiting on men self-centred and indifferent and hungry and demanding and critical, waiting for death and dying misunderstood, always behind bars, those terrifying black bars that shut us in, in the old houses, in the old city." (*VC*, p. 120) These poignant thoughts contain a rhythm of superiority, particularly when she thinks of the glory, pride and dignity of the death of the caged tiger in the zoo. Symbolically, the words are meant to be a premonition. She is not the one to sit round waiting for a meaningless death. For her the choice is between a meaningless life and non-existence, and she chooses the latter. She would prefer an end with the dignity of the tiger. Be it in the cage of her in-laws's house, it certainly would not be "melancholy as in the settling of a puff of dust upon the earth. . . . (*VC*, p. 121)

It is not enough for Monisha to feel superior to others. She must perfect her self-image of a detached person. The ideal before her is that of the *Gita* wherein she reads the qualities of a man of steady wisdom. She calls it "my book." But, notwithstanding her attempts to read it religiously, and follow its philosophy to the last word, Monisha misses the vital essence of detachment. Non-attachment of the *Gita* is a healthy attribute. It does not advocate running away from the field of action. Rather, it emphasises forgetting the self in the action. Horney also points out that resignation in true sense is worth emulating. It leads to peace and wisdom. On the other hand, a neurotic's striving for resignation signifies a peace born out of "the absence of conflicts." In spiritual pursuits of detachment, the struggle is for higher goals. Abraham Maslow terms it "metamotivation." Hindu psychology envisages freedom from the ego involvement to the optimum degree possible. In a neurotic's solution, resignation means "giving up struggle . . . and settling for less." (*NHG*, p. 260) It is a process of curtailing life and growth. For Monisha, resignation implies shutting all the doors to life and living. Wrongly does she think that she has achieved peace. Since she has not developed a healthy self-esteem, she reaches for false glory based on neurotic pride.

Monisha cuts herself from family life and lives in an ivory tower of her pride, safe in the belief of her own significance. In the *Gita*, her attention is drawn by the lines which say that a man of wisdom is satisfied in the Self by the Self alone, and he has no desires. Erroneously, she substitutes the real self by her actualized self-image and feels assured of her non-involvement. The concept of "the Self" as mentioned in the *Gita* and referred to above, is deeper than what Monisha has taken it to be. It is the *Atman*, the *Brahman*, which in Hindu thought is the supreme principle, the supreme oneness of being. C.G. Jung also employs the term to mean that part of a new centre of personality which includes the conscious as well as the unconscious, and brings a feeling of "oneness" with life—human, animal and plant. For Horney too, self means the real self, the very core of being. The glorified or idealized image is the "false self,"[17] to use the term deployed by existential psychologist R.D. Laing. What Monisha has achieved is the "fragmented self-centred concern" for "me." Fragmentation brings out division between the observer and the observed; and division means conflict. Monisha seeks just an escape from conflict—inner as well as outer—by actualizing her image of a silent sufferer, the martyr. She builds around herself a wall of fantasy. As an inhabitant of her walled, secret world, she loses the ability to live in the moment. Her obsession is to "keep it all to yourself, a secret, quite private, all your own, to keep and *gloat* over. It will hurt so much to show." (*VC*, pp. 114-15). The supreme privacy of the self falsifies all reality for her.

The retreat into the self weakens Monisha's involvement in the living world. The rift between the observer and the observed widens and conflicts multiply. Dissociation of action from life saps away the natural, normal zest to participate in life, to live and not merely to exist. Her silent advice to her brother is, "cast away involvement . . . cast it away and be totally empty, totally alone." (*VC*, p. 129) This unvoiced pleading is more for herself than for Nirode. Being "totally empty" cannot provide an answer to life's problems. Such an open contempt for life is manifest in Dostoevsky's underground hero. But then, it also implies living in a hole, or in a "glass cubicle" as Monisha realises it later. Ihab Hassan points out, in his brilliant discussion of the modern self in recoil, that the cult of inactivity involves the "alienation of the moral and artistic imagination from things of this world, often leading to a criminal state of autonomy."[18] In fact, a balance is to be maintained in, what Ortega Y. Gasset calls "the other" and the retreat into the self. Monisha's failure to maintain the equilibrium, heightens her will-lessness, which in turn, implies a rejection of life. What she achieves is just a sealing up of aspirations.

By negating healthy aspirations, Monisha has lost the will to accept challenges of life. Her conscience is withered and dead. She disdains anything that may draw her into the ring. "Allow us just this—to stand back, apart, in the shadows, and watch the fire and the flames, the sacrifices that are flung into it . . . and permit us—*not to take part.*" (*VC*, p. 136) Here she speaks for herself and Nirode. For Monisha, as also for Nirode, touch and communication imply a humiliation. She wishes to stay solitary and work alone: "Alone, I would work better and I should feel whole."

This urge to "feel whole" is not wholesome, but an outcome of a desire to shut all doors. Amla notices the change in her sister—not physical but something "seemed to have seized the girl and turned her inside out, giving her eery unreality. Something, Amla saw, had laid its hands upon her, scarred and altered her till she bore only the faintest resemblance to the quiet and subtly uncaring elder sister Amla had remembered." (*VC*, p. 142) Anita Desai employs the metaphor of the city to convey the two selves of Monisha. The city—Calcutta—has two faces: one rapacious, the other weary. Likewise, Monisha has two selves—one "glorified," the other actual. Her actual self is weary; the glorified is rapacious. Her real self is symbolised by the Bleeding Heart Dove—caged and wounded. Just as the dove is not bleeding, it only has a scar, her real self is also not suffering because it is exiled. Her false self suffers. Another suggestive imagery is that of the criss-cross bar and the windows. Physically, she is trapped behind these; psychologically, her real self is shut behind the barred exigencies of her glorified self. This image becomes clearer in the last scene when she struggles to establish a rapport with her banished real self. When charged of theft Monisha's glorified self suffers, her image receives a shattering blow.

It can be argued that even a relatively normal and healthy person will resent an allegation of theft. The difference, however, lies in their typical responses. A healthy person may feel hurt, shocked or infuriated, but he will not be irrational in his claims as a neurotic does. Monisha's need to "be always *right*," entitles her never to be doubted. All this while, she has strived to feel superior to her in-laws. Now, under the pressure of the accusation, her glorified self-image crumbles down. It is unbearable "to be regarded so low by men and women themselves so low" (*VC*, p. 136); this thought speaks of her disdain. She gets yet another shock at the realisation that she does not belong to the household. This works at the unconscious level, although at the conscious level she has never belonged to Jiban's family. His words, "why didn't you tell me before you took it ?" (*VC*, p. 138) cut her even deeper. Gripped by neurotic claims and inner dictates, she traverses "the whole range of anxiety, despair, self-condemnation and self-destructive impulses." (*NHG*, p. 74)

Being a withdrawn type, Monisha's first automatic impulse is to save her face by "exile" into her shell. As solitude suits her temperament, she willingly accepts to live there "a little beyond and below everyone else, in exile." (*VC*, p. 136) This is a way to restore her pride. The urge to hide is ingrained in her. It is presented symbolically as the desire to "dive" underground in the lanes of Calcutta; but, just as the burroughs are overpopulated, so is Jiban's home. She always thinks of it as Jiban's home, not her. After the charge of theft, aloofness suits her. Locked in her room, she reads books and feels self-important. At night, she creeps up the top-most floor and enjoys a communion with vast, dark emptiness. This is her hour of freedom. But, what she considers freedom is just a flight from conflict. Real freedom implies cessation of all conflict and liberation from all fear.[19] Monisha has not achieved it. She fears the aggressiveness of her in-laws. She undergoes a tremendous amount of psychological tussle. She does not get freedom because she does not acquire self-knowledge.

Only a brief moment of self-discovery enables Monisha to know her real self in the brilliant black eyes of the street dancer. Suddenly, she is scared that a "glance of those enormous and brilliant black eyes would dissolve and disintegrate her into a meaningless shadow." (*VC*, p. 237) This is her glorified self, afraid of disintegration in the encounter with true self. As the rustic dancers beat their drums, she awakens to a greater truth about her life: she has so far led a barred, enclosed existence devoid of all human feelings. The truth unveils still greater reality that her life has been a waste. A terrible struggle ensues between her glorified and real selves. There is a frenzied search for feelings and emotions. So far, Monisha's gaze was directed inward but its centre was false. Now, in the light of the outer world, she comprehends the inner reality. All her "grandiose fantasies" about herself as a detached person of "steady wisdom" perish. Self-hate emerges with the realization that she has been an escapist. She has run away from the realm of feelings. Her unproductive life, lived in a "steel container," (like Beckett's hero in *The Unnamable* living in a jar), appears detestable. So far, she has lacked human warmth. She reproaches herself: "These people know and feel something I do not." The consciousness of having been emotionally crippled and the inability to share feelings with others on human level, isolate her. The dagger is turned inward. Pure violence erupts as an ultimate form of introspection. As R.D. Laing points out, such "isolation is greatly in danger of passing over into psychotic alienation."[20]

On introspection Monisha is terrified by her emotional vacuum. This new awareness leaves her guilty when judged by her true self. Like the Hunter Gracchus of Kafka, she seems to be in a rudderless ship, driven by the wind that blows in the undermost regions of death. The consciousness of inadequacy is painful and grotesque. If, as Dostoevsky says, "every sort of consciousness . . . is a disease," then the only course open to eliminate ourselves is to strike at our own individuality. Just as Maya's self is reflected in the mirror, Monisha's self flashes in the eyes of the dancer. In self-hate Maya strikes a her mirrored image to kill it, Monisha only gnashes her teeth because she cannot hit the dancer's eyes. Here, we are reminded of Dorian Gray, who, in self-hate, stabs his own picture to "kill this monstrous soul-life," because without its hideous warnings, he would be at peace."[21]

Monisha's self-hate turns into a self-destructive impulse. So intense are her feelings that she despises the idea of being herself. This can be termed as terror of having a clear perception of her identity. Her self-hate is symbolised by the personification of the dancer woman as *Kali*, representing destructive forces. Kali also stands for nature's totality: destruction being an intrinsic part of nature's procreative process. This is a brief moment of introspection for Monisha. She suffers intensely. Suffering could lead to self-analysis and to intentionality, which according to Rollo May, is the preconscious process that gives a person orientation. But, for Monisha this moment is too short to allow any constructive thinking. Overpowered by self-pity and self-reproach, she feels like Sartre's Roquentin, "My thought is me. . . . At this very moment—it's frightful—if I exist, it is because I am horrified at existence."[22] Humiliated by her inability to respond "to passion with passion, to sorrow with sorrow," Monisha feels entrapped. She is scared; scared of "the great empty white distance set between her and this moist, crimson flowering of emotion in the street below." (*VC*, p. 238) The vision of herself, in the light of the reality, is grotesquely unbearable. She sets fire to herself to end the despised real self. It is significant to note that Maya is led to self-destructive urges out of frustration at not finding "life," Monisha commits suicide out of despair at not being able to experience life. In both these cases self-hate turns into self-destruction. Two forces work havoc with these young women: the albino priest and Calcutta city. These images correspond to the evil magician and the witch, "Spenser's Archimago and Duessa."[23]

Anita Desai's women, though apparently sitting and waiting for something to happen, as Sita does in *Where Shall We Go This Summer?* or Pat in the short story "Scholar and Gypsy," are spirited enough to take life in their hands and struggle to acquire a new awareness in order to protect their integrity as human beings. Sita goes to the island and gains a new vision; Pat decides to forsake her futile cocktail parties to find a positive meaning in existence. Monisha opts for a violent end to establish her triumph over her in-laws by defeating their attempts to subjugate her. This is a neurotic way to feel "great" and "free." It denotes an unconscious impulse "to frustrate, outwit or defeat others in personal relations." (*NHG*, p. 27)

Maya, in *Cry, the Peacock*, is Anita Desai's first character study of a woman torn between the inner and outer reality, between her conception of life as "Elysian lawns," and life as it really is,—hard, harsh, protean, full of mediocrity. She is a brilliantly documented figure, portraying an alienated consciousness, tortured by her own phobias and neurosis. In her earnest appeal for love, her child-like responses to life's problems and hypersensitivity, she is an inhabitant more of a fantastic realm than the world of everyday reality. Curiously enough, Maya is a tragic predecessor of Monisha of *Voices in the City*. These two stand at the head of a long line of protagonists—Nirode, Nanda, Sita, Sarah, Amla, Bim and Deven—who indicate a steady progress in their march from self-alienation to self-discovery, from there to self-actualization, from sickness to health, from neurosis to "full humanness." While Maya and Monisha spell their own destruction by their refusal to see, accept and live the ordinariness of life, some of Desai's later characters realise that acceptance of existence will lead to fulfilment through affirmative self-abandonment, not through destructive self-abnegation.

## NOTES

1. R.S. Sharma, *Anita Desai*, p. 25.
2. Madhusudan Prasad, *Anita Desai: The Novelist*.
3. Ann Lowry Weir, "The Illusions of Maya: Feminine Consciousness in Anita Desai's *Cry, the Peacock*," *Journal of South Asian Literature*, 21, No. 2 (Summer-Fall, 1981), pp. 1-4.

4. Jasbir Jain, *Stairs to the Attic*, p. 117.
5. "Anita Desai," in *Indian English Novelists*, ed. Madhusudan Prasad (New Delhi: Sterling, 1982).
6. B. Ramachandra Rao, "Themes and Variations in the Novels and Short Stories of Anita Desai," *Journal of Literature and Aesthetics*, 2, Nos. 2-3 (April-July 1982), pp. 74-79.
7. J. Krishnamurthy, *Beyond Violence* (London: Victor Gallenez, 1973), p. 39.
8. Abraham Maslow, *The Farther Reaches of Human Nature* (Harmandsworth: Pelican, 1971), p. 117. Hereafter cited in text as *FRHN*, along with pagination.
9. Erich Fromm, *Escape from Freedom*, p. 174.
10. Feodor Dostoevsky, *Notes from Underground* in *Notes from Underground, White Nights, The Dream of a Ridiculous Man and Sections from the House of the Dead*, trans. Andrew R. MacAndrew (London: New American Library, A Signet Classic, 1961), p. 199.
11. Erich Fromm, *The Art of Loving* (1957; rpt. London: Unwin Paperbacks, 1976), p. 105.
12. Virginia Woolf, *A Writer's Diary* (1953; rpt. New York: New American Library, 1968), Oct. 14, 1922, p. 52.
13. Virginia Woolf, *The Waves* (1931; rpt. London: Hogarth, 1963), p. 46.
14. Arun Joshi, *The Last Labyrinth* (New Delhi: Orient Paperbacks, 1981).
15. B. Ramachandra Rao, *Anita Desai*.
16. Meena Shirwadkar, *Images of Women in Indo-Anglian Novel* (New Delhi: Sterling, 1979), p. 64.
17. R.D. Laing, *The Divided Self* (1960; rpt. Harmondsworth: Penguin, 1973).
18. Ihab Hassan, *Radical Innocence* (Princeton: Princeton University Press, 1961), p. 28.
19. J. Krishnamurthy points out that unless "the mind is absolutely free from fear every form of action brings

**about more mischief, more misery, more confusion."** ***Beyond Violence*, p. 31.**

20. *The Divided Self*, p. 140.
21. Oscar Wilde, *The Picture of Dorian Gray*, in *The Works of Oscar Wilde* (1948; rpt. London: Collins, 1969), p. 167.
22. Jean-Paul Sartre, *Nausea*, trans. Robert Baldick (Harmondsworth: Penguin, 1966), p. 135.
23. Northrop Frye, *Anatomy of Criticism* (New Jersey: Princeton, 1957), p. 196.

# 4

# THE IMMEASURABLE EMPTINESS

If Maya and Monisha represent moments of crisis during which the self has to choose between life and death, Nirode in *Voices in the City*, and Nanda Kaul and Raka in *Fire on the Mountain* reveal those self-alienating tendencies that hasten their self-destructive moves. They cannot make decisions, assume responsibility and direct their lives. They adopt compounded solutions to cope with their problems. Nirode, for example, is a victim of an intra-psychic conflict wherein his expansive and resigned drives clash. When one solution fails to relieve his inner tension, he tries another. Nanda and Raka run away from social and familial ties and maintain an attitude of resignation. They bargain for peace by fleeing conflicts. Despite these basic differences in their solutions, each of the three characters loses his or her identity, becomes depersonalized, asserts a false image and gives in to neurosis.

## I

Nirode is the chief protagonist of *Voices in the City*. A Kafkaesque figure, he is the "self" that is ever alone despite its continuous search for connection. There is an obsessive repetitive quality in his terror of happiness and suffering and his existential "angst" of the abyss of the self. Some critics find in him a character "deeply influenced" by Camus, Kafka, Baudelaire, and tend to see him as a figure who has walked out of the pages of one of Camus's novels. It is pointed out that Nirode's experiments with failures are an indication of a "quest for an abiding meaning in life." He achieves nothing in the end and remains a rootless drifter who can neither compromise with the world nor reject it as absurd like Camus's Meursault. Another critic argues that Nirode is an introverted romantic. He cannot become a torch-bearer of a true revolutionary spirit. He abuses his intellect in the name of freedom and goes to seed. "He is caught in a kind of intellectual vice. . . . There is something hollow, something phoney about his protestations and diatribes."[1]

Whereas some critics have studied Nirode's Hamletian disgust and Lawrentian Oedipus complex, it is arguable that his difficulties do not arise out of sexual urges in the Freudian sense. In Horneyan terms, Nirode does not strive for freedom in the manner of a healthy individual, but tries to adopt the strategy of withdrawal so as to escape conflicts. A deeper probing into the workings of his mind will show the psychological causes behind the dislocation of his psyche. Nirode, the "congenital failure" goes astray while searching for his glorified self. If aunt Lila finds him a disgusting bohemian, Monisha thinks of him lovingly "as a broken bird . . . in the aviary." (*VC*, p. 125) These images do not redeem the personality of a man suffering under the conflicting demands of his psyche.

As Nirode's basic needs have been frustrated, he alienates himself from his essential nature; his value system is damaged. He accepts neurotic values, thereby developing neurotic wants which are destructive, both for self and for others. Bernard J. Paris underlines the importance of Maslow's value theory and points out that some values are healthy whereas some are neurotic. All values derive from human wants; but while healthy basic needs are "conducive to a fuller realization of human potential," neurotic wants are destructive. "Frustration of the basic needs so alienates the individual from his essential nature and so disturbs the course of his development that he is no longer aware of his own best interests or able to pursue them."[2]

The condition for and the symptoms of anxiety take roots in Nirode's home. Anita Desai touches upon their childhood and displays how well she intuits the causes of self-alienation in early stages. The isolation and hostility of their apparently happy home work towards emotional imbalance of the three siblings. Equipped with class, money, taste and intellectuality, this home suffers with an inner deficiency which creates a strange mass of dark forces within, to combat with. The most damaging situation arises when the children notice open hostility and contempt between their parents. Their indolent, weak-willed and idle father has an unconcealed malice for his wife; their accomplished, polished but dominating mother reveals her disdain and resentment towards her spouse. The mute sufferers of this tension are the children. They have no "room to grow" as a child-psychologist puts it. Bringing up children is a difficult art. It "involves working with an unusual medium, one that has a mind and will of its own, a child who is constantly his own designer."[3] In order to help the child in his process of self-creation, the parents must enter into a partnership with him. Nirode's parents woefully lack this involvement. Their personal prejudices—"terrible contempt and resentment," in mother's eyes, the malice and spite in father's smile—seep into their young lives. They fail to grow as self-directed individuals. The worst sufferer is Nirode, the eldest.

As if the tension between his parents is not damaging enough, Nirode falls a prey to another detrimental condition: partiality. His father altogether neglects him, and reposes a greater confidence in Arun, his favourite. The first few pages of the novel smack of Nirode's malice; he is "corroded with hate" (*VC*, p. 7) for Arun. Even Amla, the youngest of them all, notices father's bias and later she tells Dharma, father "was imperiously unfair" (*VC*, p. 207) to Nirode. Consequently, Nirode starts losing his "basic-confidence" and turns a "congenital failure." The term "basic confidence" is used by Marie Rasey to mean confidence in others and in self. A child who grows up in a congenial "atmosphere of confidence, encouragement in his activities, and constructive discipline," (*NHG*, p. 86) and who gets warmth and a feeling of security develops it along with healthy self-respect. Instead, Nirode's "inner strength and coherence" is sapped by self-pity. One may have a glimpse of his emotional state in his nostalgic thoughts. After bidding farewell to Arun, Nirode broods over his unfortunate boyhood: only if he had been a promising lad, he would have sailed to England for higher studies instead of Arun.

> It might have been he, he knew that, had he not, as a child, an emotional and disorderly schoolboy, fallen from his horse and declared to his father, through tears, that he hated horses, sports and would never ride again. . . . If Arun had not ridden like a prince, captained the cricket team and won top honours in all examinations. If his father, while dictating his will to an obese solicitor, had not weighed these distinctions before laying aside a sum of money for the education of one of his two sons. If Arun had not been the favourite and Nirode a congenital failure. (*VC*, pp. 7-8)

To cope with his basic anxiety generated by his uncertain childhood, Nirode adopts first the "move away from others." (*NHG*, p. 19) He shuts others from his life and becomes detached. He has learnt early in life that he can escape inner turmoil if he frees himself from all wishes, ambitions, emotional ties and efforts for achievement. This tantamounts to rejecting life as such. He glories in his failures, detachment and emptiness. At the same time, his expansive drives prove stronger than his moves away from people. The basic necessity of his temperament is to weild power over others; he must master life; he must rebel and fight to maintain his grandiose image of himself. Under the expansive solution, one sub-type, listed by Horney is that of an "arrogant-vindictive" personality. Such a person is identified with his pride. The motivating force in his life is his need for vindictive triumph. Nirode's entire move in life is to frustrate and humiliate others which reveals his neurotic need to be a dictatorial figure amid his friends and well-wishers. He takes pride in himself for his stoical attitude towards life in general and his family in particular. He comes to believe that he has "done with everything . . . given up talking and telling." (*VC*, p. 130) With his mouth sealed up and ears clogged, he presumes that he is blissfully at peace. This belief is as erroneous as that of his sister, Monisha's. Nirode and Monisha do not understand that lack of communication and the loss of self-world relationship only create an emotional and spiritual wasteland.

Fears of personal inferiority lead Nirode to search for glory: first by being an out-law and then by priding himself as an "ill-tempered hermit." In real life, he cannot be on par with his brother Arun—neither in academic field nor in extra-curricular activities. This is insulting. He feels unwanted, isolated and belittled. The unconscious mental processes devise ways and means to surmount this inadequacy. As a boy, he achieves this by running away from home several times. Being searched for and brought back home elevate his position in his own eyes. That he belongs to them, that he is wanted, is in itself an anxiety-relieving feeling. Thus he manages to get the much-needed parental attention which he otherwise fails to attract. An aggressive child, as Horney observes, places "value on strength and on the capacity to endure and fight." (*NHG*, p. 20)

This aggressiveness and the desire for vindictive triumph precisely delineates the adult character of Nirode: conscious of his poverty, the self-inflicted troubles and the urge for failure, yet possessed of a Promethean pride in his endurance and strength coupled with the ability to fight. Unfortunately, Nirode is neither a Prometheus, nor the hero of the age-old myth of the Symplegades, crossing through the jaws of death to the other world and immortality. He is a distraught young man with a conspicuous desire for failure. W. Hale White dramatises the theme of "perpetual rise" in one of his books. He maintains that the law of the Universe is "the perpetual rise from the lower to the higher; an immortality of aspiration after more perfect type; a suppression and happy forgetfulness of its comparative failure."[4] These are the characteristics of a healthy man possessed of deep aspirations. Conversely, Nirode longs for a fall deep down the bottomless rock; he wants failure after failure so that he does not have to bear the burden of success. In saner moments, he realises that his boyish escapades have been a nightmare, not a real journey, because he has never been able to start, to take the first step forward.

Nirode's inability to start a journey denotes the basic uncertainties in his temperament. He likes to sink comfortably into the effortless inevitability of the betrayed man. His real self is exiled and in its stead, there is the false 'I' operating. The centre of the realm of experience—the self—is absent. While the urge to start the journey assumes, intermittently, almost pathological proportions, it is a mark of his lack of volition that he is powerless to act and set out on his journey. The novelist points out:

> The suitcase is never packed, the tickets never purchased, and the ship sails, leaving one ensnared in the net of sleep. He was not one of those born with a destination balanced like a boiled egg upon a silver spoon in his mouth. He was merely a traveller and the only reasonable thing to do was to accept the journeying as meaningful in itself. (*VC*, p. 10)

Nirode lacks—to use Erikson's phrase—autonomy, individuation. D.H. Lawrence, in "The Crown" describes such a self:

> The darkness, having overcome the light, reaching the dead null wall of the womb, reacts into self-consciousness, and recoils upon itself. At the same time, the light has surpassed its limits, becomes conscious, and starts its reflex to recoil upon itself. Thus the false 'I' comes into being: the I which thinks itself supreme and infinite, and which is, in fact, sick foetus shut up in the walls of an unrelaxed womb.[5]

His wish to begin the journey is just a desire to escape. With the whistle of the train or hooter of the ship, he hears the call "escape, escape." Physically, he has managed to come a long way from his stifling childhood environment, but it is not an answer to his problem. There is satisfaction when one reaches a goal. But, for Nirode there is no goal to reach to. He is being tossed about by his struggle to hold on to his identity. Human wish is a propelling force which includes both memory and fantasy and "is the beginning of orienting ourselves to the future, an admission that we *want* the future to be such and such; it is a capacity to reach down deep into ourselves with a longing to change the future."[6] Nirode's wish is engaged in his search for an idealized image.

Nirode idealizes himself in two images—one, that of an independent person free of all ties: familial, social or emotional; and second, that of a hero who would rise in spite of his failures. This is a typical characteristic whereby the neurotic is not motivated by his wishes but by his needs emerging from his pride system. This is "the shift of energies from developing the given potentials of the real self to developing the fictitious potentials of the idealized self." (*NHG*, p. 166) By denying his past, his family name and claim to property, he asserts his freedom. This disavowal is an attempt of the self to create its own identity with nothing but its own volition. But Nirode does not have a "will," only an emptiness and a vacuity to fill in. To David he speaks of his longing to do away with "happiness and suffering . . . disregard them, see beyond them to the very end." (*VC*, p. 40) Gradually, he learns to look at himself as a person "for whom aloneness alone was the sole natural condition, aloneness alone the treasure worth treasuring." (*VC*, p. 24)

Nirode's ardent desire, throughout the novel, is to fail at everything. It is a negative attitude. However, Nirode adopts it in order to fill in the unbearable vacuum created in him since childhood. In his idealized self-image Nirode becomes a hero, a modern Sisyphus, rolling the boulder uphill. What he tells David is significant from psychological perspective;

> I want to move from failure to failure to failure, step by step to rock bottom. I want to explore that depth. When you climb a ladder, all you find at the top is space, all you can do is leap off—fall to the bottom. I want to get there without that meaningless climbing. I want to descend quickly. (*VC*, p. 40)

To fail and to start on a new project gives him, in a way, heroic dimensions. That he regards himself as a hero is substantiated by the text. After the above statement on failure, he quotes Camus. It cannot be denied that Camus and Sisyphus are working deep down his sub-conscious. It is arguable, nevertheless, that Nirode's desire to avoid climbing up is in itself a denial of Sisyphus-image. But, the yearning to fail quickly in order to start afresh, denotes the process of climbing up. Further, authorial intrusion, "how the young can believe in their attitudes, till the attitude becomes the self" (*VC*, p. 40) indicates the glorified image becoming the glorified self. David chides Nirode for his defeatist tendencies and interprets it as "absolute negation."

David's assessment is correct to an extent. Nirode's scorn of success is partly a negation of a world wherein he feels isolated, and partly a passivity of will due to lack of basic self-confidence. Faith in self and in others is an essential attribute of real self-esteem. Nirode realises in rare moments of introspection, "this lack of faith and this questioning," (*VC*, p. 39) is his undoing. Unfortunately, this realization remains only at the level of discussion. It is not strong enough to afford him self-analysis which could divert his energies towards health. The essence of his problem is aimlessness, fear and a blocking off of consciousness. Human life, says Buber, is life in dialogue, and we can know the self only through it. This presupposes a communication between the consciousness of individuals. Since Nirode has no "I-Thou" communion he cannot develop inter-personal empathy.

Man defines himself in relation to the outside world; he grasps his identity in others. In his novel *Island*, Aldous Huxley describes Will Farnaby's moment of revelation when he sees the "Suchness" of the world in the blazing bush:

> . . . the fact remained and would remain always, remain everywhere—the fact that there was this capacity even in a paranoiac for intelligence, even in a devil-worshipper for love; the fact that the ground of all being could be totally manifest in a flowering shrub, a human face; the fact that there was a light and that this light was also compassion.[7]

The experience of being blissfully one with oneness, as Huxley points out, is healthy relatedness. It is achieved when the sense of self is securely established. Nirode has no sense of real self. He is losing contact with reality. All his efforts are diverted towards preserving his identity. In Nirode's character, Anita Desai shows her prowess of a powerful dramatization of human isolation. Dissatisfied with his family and society, Nirode seeks solace in his self-conceived world of imagination. Erik H. Erickson uses the term "negative identity" for the state in which the 'I' is burdened down rendering an individual unable to participate in speciation. In Nirode's case, his real self, the 'I' is not encumbured; it is shunted out by his super-ego, i.e. his glorified self-image. Consequently, he cannot arrive at a correct self-definition. He is certain that one can retain one's sanity by being secretive and closing all communication. To Monisha he exhorts, "Never tell them your secret." (*VC*, p. 132) Communion appears to him painful and humiliating as to Monisha. "I made myself inferior to all these frauds by making an attempt to make them read anything I'd written. Anything that is of any value to oneself should be kept Great Secret," (*VC*, p. 132) he tells her. Later, the same idea is elaborated during his encounter with Amla. He asserts that his whole life is a process of preserving his conscience:

> . . . the only thing I wanted to protect, what any sane man needs protect, is his conscience. Oh, individuality you might call it, or conscience, or as I do, or anything—but there must be this essence inside you, and you must keep it secret in order to keep it—bearable. Mixing, diluting, muddying it—that's the disease. (*VC*, p. 184)

Ironically, Nirode takes offence at the word "morbid" for his life-style. He springs up in defence and tells Amla that he has passed every "stage of morbidity in order to arrive at this state of health." (*VC*, p. 183) For him, living as he does, in a rat hole, a parasite on friends, being secretive, is health.

Paradoxically enough, what Nirode considers sanity and health is just the reverse of it. R. D. Laing aptly terms it "ontological insecurity." When an individual has a firm sense of other people's reality and identity, he feels real, alive and whole. He is an ontologically secure individual. He can encounter the difficulties of life with validating certainties. On the contrary, an ontologically insecure person feels "more dead than alive." His autonomy and identity are uncertain. He gets absorbed in finding ways and means to feel alive. He is immersed in himself and appears stoical, indifferent and withdrawn; "the world of his experience comes to be one he can no longer share with other people."[10]

Withdrawal is an important solution Nirode adopts to counter the difficulties generated by his "ontological insecurities." In the first few pages of the novel we learn that he has opted for a life of "shadows, silence and stillness." (*VC*, p. 8) This is a defence mechanism to guard his idealized self-image as a self-sufficient and independent individual. Certainly, it is not the healthy striving for inner silence during which Coleridge's "the unobtrusive song of Happiness," is heard. Dr. Radhakrishnan thinks that silent hours give us time for self-communication which can lead to self-analysis. "In these silent hours . . . we strive to free ourselves from the suffocating routine, from the masks and mummeries of existence, cleanse our thoughts and create within ourselves a clean heart and a single mind."[11] Nirode creates for himself dead silence. It does not vibrate with the voice of the spirit. It is not a sign of normal withdrawal but a neurotic compulsion. J. Krishnamurthy also observes that silence is not absence of noise. It is a higher virtue requiring the sound foundation of love. "If you have not laid the foundation, which is love, which is virtue, which is goodness, which is beauty, which is real compassion in the depth of your whole being, if you have not done that, your silence is only the ending of noise."[12] Nirode's life-pattern is a negation of all beauty, goodness and compassion. He is sick and he is aware of it: "I am a leper . . . leave me, do not come near. I am a leper, diseased with the loneliest disease of all." (*VC*, p. 61) Nirode can be compared with Dostoevsky's underground man. Both are sick and both glorify it because they live with it. As Bernard J. Paris points out, the underground man is diseased but "his disease is that of being 'too conscious' (i, ii), too intelligent; and it places him far above the stupid normal men of action whom he so envies and so despises."[11] Likewise Nirode's self-conscious superiority and his repulsion for all normal men is evident in the novel.

Nirode is jealous not only of Arun but of all those who follow a routine. The thought of being one with the office-going crowd repels him:

> Revulsion filled him, so huge a distaste and horror filled him that he felt empowered by it—as Arun, who did not know it, would never be empowered—to rise like a clumsy paper kite with a candle lit inside it that rises above the sooty chimney pots and crooked pigeon-roosts to fly, fly through an immensity of air—above Arun in his crawling train, above the painted ship on the sluggish river, intoxicatingly light and free and powerful. (*VC*, p. 10)

The appeal of freedom and the strategy of mastery, as expressed in the last line of the above quotation, are the two most important solutions of Nirode. He edifies his detachment. He tells Bose, with the characteristic casualness of a grandiose person, that he has not resigned his job with the *Patrika*; but, "I am simply not going there." (*VC*, p. 15) He overlooks the future implications of being unemployed. The fear of starvation or the humiliation of having to borrow from friends is comparatively insignificant against the compulsive neurotic urge to be free of all routine.

As a detached person, Nirode cannot work under others. It is "impossible, physically impossible to work under any man, by his orders, at a given time, at a meaningless job. I loathe those automatons at the top—I loathe their superciliousness, their *blindness*." (*VC*, p. 18) This statement matches the description Horney gives of the difficulties faced by detached persons in their work. Such individuals can work better alone. Since Nirode is sensitive to coercion, it is difficult for him to work for a boss or under rules and regulations. In order to work in a free atmosphere, he starts his magazine, *Voice*. Apparently, it is given to understand that *Voice* will cater to intellectuals and will serve art. This is a make-believe. In fact, it only feeds Nirode's vanity.

The magazine, however, does not provide Nirode the desired freedom. It requires communications, contacts and competitiveness. Since Nirode controls all aspirations and wishes, he lacks competitive spirit. Contracts and communications horrify him. Monetary assistance could come from many sources, particularly from his mother, who will open up her coffers for him:

> But the habit of withdrawal had become too strong . . . Nirode grew more and more wary of contact. . . . The intricacies of relationship—approach, recompense, obligation—these aroused in him violent distaste and kept him hovering on the fringe of the world that invited and spurned by turns, and for which he daily cared less. (*VC*, p. 62)

The magazine becomes a farce. When it shows some signs of revival, Nirode abandons it. His next venture is to write a play. This also fails because he is irritated and intrigued by the expectations of others. He wishes to disown it as the most absurd thing he ever did. A sense of futility grips him and he feels flat, inert, reluctant to raise to his feet again. Starting again means putting in efforts. It tantamounts to participating in life—its activities, human contacts and ambitions, for which he has a strong dislike. He feels proud in his non-involvement, his stoicity and emptiness.

This is a false pride arising out of Nirode's neurotic claims to measure up to his inner dictates. His most imperative need is to elevate himself in his own eyes. He gains this by rejecting all help from his mother, aunt Lila, Jit and some of his friends. If he accepts their aid, he may be acknowledging them. If he succeeds in life, he may be just another individual—one of the multitudes. In his eyes, he is someone special, a dignitary in his own sense on whom friends dote. At the unconscious level, it is the reversal of values. He transforms his rebellion against family and society into virtues. His arrogance turns into his philosophic rage, his rudeness, and artist's temper, and his frustration, the sign of an intellectual restlessness. He succeeds in creating for himself a personality—an invulnerable individual, a self-righteous and angry prince who throws away a huge property for his principles.

Is Nirode a stoic ? Is he really beyond all pain ? No. It is Nirode's self-deception. He is an "unshelled snail," "a broken bird," as Monisha often thinks of him. However unfeeling, rude and ill-tempered he may pose to be, he is essentially high-strung. He cannot tolerate other's opinions; he reacts with vengeance to criticism. It may be argued that even a healthy person resents criticism and injury to his pride. But, there is a sharp difference between the two. A normal person's pride is based on "substantial attributes," of his personality, such as feeling of quiet dignity at having achieved something in life, or, a comprehensive feeling of regard for some personal value or act. Neurotic pride, on the contrary, stands on "shaky" grounds. It rests on the idealized image. Nirode's need to be a hero drives him to arrogant retaliation.

Nirode's reactions, even to ordinary, harmless suggestions given by Sonny, Bose or Jit, are violent and insolent; and baffle the readers. Two causes work behind these reactions: Nirode's "arrogant-vindictive" drives and his pride-system. As an arrogant-vindictive sub-type, he derives satisfaction by achieving vindictive triumph. It also manifests itself in his violent rages and his contemptuous disregard for others. In normal human relations vengeance and triumph are kept under control by three factors: love, fear and self-preservation. They act as checks. When these checks are "malfunctioning can the vindictiveness involve the total personality—thereby becoming a kind of integrating force, as in Medea—and sway it altogether in the one direction of vengeance and triumph." (*NHG*, p. 198) Nirode's life shows a stark deficiency of the three ingredients mentioned above. For self-preservation he humiliates others. Some glaring examples can be found in the manner he insults Sonny and Bose, the way he ridicules the contributors to his magazine. This makes him feel triumphant. When his friends place their hopes and trust in *Voice* Nirode enjoys closing down the magazine, so that he can frustrate their expectations. It affords him a sense of achievement to use them as a means to his victory. Not that he really is marching towards a solid goal; letting down others is elevating enough in itself. It confirms his power over them. This indicates his lack of sympathy for others and for himself. The second question, that of neurotic pride, also figures in here. Nirode humiliates his friends because they hurt his pride by supporting him during his period of unemployment. At the unconscious level he knows that he has to depend on them and that he is not self-sufficient as he glories himself to be. The victims of his shame and subsequent wrath are: Sonny, who alternately feeds his ego by his devotion but hurts it by feeding him; David who arouses excessive shame in him by his self-effacing simplicity; and Jit, because he is a "boxwallah."

The reasons why Nirode often insults Jit, are complicated. Jit belongs to a strata of society which Nirode professes to hate but unconsciously yearns for. This longing defeats him as he cannot resist Jit and his world. He falls a prey to his own intra-psychic conflicts and combats his helplessness by being rude, and insulting. Once, under the effect of wine, Jit comes out with a surprising revelation and tells Nirode a truth which the latter perhaps tries to camouflage behind his roughness. Jit tells Nirode that all his anger against the "boxwallahs" is owing to his dormant craving to be one of them and lead their life of comforts:

> You rant against us precisely because you realize our danger —we entice you. We hover in the foreground like an oasis—and once you've done your little stint of adventuring in the desert, you'll get very thirsty. So thirsty you will drink anything—anything that resembles the patriarchal security and comfort and the matriarchal indulgence that you broke away from, so boldly and recklessly. (*VC*, pp. 97-98)

It is to be noted that instead of getting worked up in his usual way at this harsh truth, Nirode is candid for once: "why don't I give it all up and go abck to her ? She'd put me on my feet again, and I'd probably find it a relief to be on them again instead of lurching about on my knees and tipping over on to my head every so often." (*VC*, p. 102)

Till Monisha's death, whatever pain is experienced remains at the superficial level of the pseudo-self. Monisha's suicide and mother's subsequent attitude affect him in a devastating way. In the reality and intensity of his suffering he discovers his vulnerability: that he is not a stoic, beyond pain or pleasure; that he has not done away with family ties and deeper feelings; that he can be touched by personal grief. So long he has been successful in self-deceit, considering himself immune from "the torment of conscience." He describes it as a "drugged, dull sleep in which he had rocked obliviously for so many years . . . scornful of his success, stagnant and dehydrated of all ambition, communion, relationship, joy and responsibility. (*VC*, p. 250) During this period of family tragedy, the foundation of his false self is shaken, affording him a glimpse of his inner self. He awakens to the necessity of exploring within himself the essential experience of love and affection. What he had lacked so far was the exercise of his ability to love in an outgoing concern for the welfare of others, sharing their pleasures and pains. A communion of consciousness with others can now have a constructive effect on him.

Horney opines that real suffering has a therapeutic effect on an individual: it has the power "to broaden and deepen our range of feelings and to open our hearts for the sufferings of others." (*NHG*, p. 163) For a brief duration Nirode experiences a communication with his real self in the hour of agony. He regains his human capacity to sympathise with Amla and aunt Lila in their suffering. In these moments of inter-personal empathy and tenderness, he reaches out to them, shares their feelings and is filled with tenderness for the world.

> . . . he was filled with an immense care of the world that made him reach out, again and again, to touch Amla's cold hand. . . . He pressed them to him with hunger and joy, as if he rejoiced in this sensation of touching other flesh, others' pains, longed to make them mingle with his own, which till now had been agonisingly neglected. (*VC*, p. 248)

Nirode turns into a reflective person who can divert the energies of his self to enlarge its preceptiveness. This is an elevating experience for Nirode. He can see the whole pattern of life and death, "the whole fantastic design of . . . incarnation followed by reincarnation, of unconsciousness turning into consciousness, of sleep followed by waking." (*VC*, p. 249)

Unfortunately, this experience does not liberate Nirode. He cannot integrate the fragments of his inner and outer worlds to give meaning to his existence. He cannot free himself from the entanglement of his false vanity. Conflicting forces work on his psyche triggering off the process of deterioration. Rejection by his doting mother deals a severe blow to Nirode's pride. It is insulting to be so discarded and further it hurts him to realise that he is not yet ready for absolute freedom. Self-contempt and self-hate grip him. Their mother accepts Monisha's death stoically. She has thus achieved what Nirode has failed to. He hates his mother for it and then directs this despise towards himself. Severe self-hate leads to self-destructive tendencies.

The emergence of mother *Kali* in his psyche is symbolic of the deteriorating process. The danger-signals of self-destructiveness appear in the form of symbols such as demons, monsters or ghosts. *Kali* reprsents the dark half of female totality. She is the principle of destruction as well as pro-creation. Here, cultural factors play an important rôle. *Kali* is the mother goddess of Bengal in particular and of India in general. She remains in the "collective unconscious" of the race. There are incidents in Swami Vivekananda's life when Mother *Kali* converged into his psyche. Nirode too belongs to Bengal. In his moments of crisis the real and the archetypal fuse into one in his imagination.

Nirode's chaotic state of mind indicates the terror of the dark unknown: Death. He tells Amla that he has been sentenced to death. "I am prepared and waiting for it. I have heard her approach—death, Kali . . . while she watches I grow more and more vividly alive by the minute, and also closer and closer to my death." (*VC*, p. 256) Nirode recognises the duality: knowledge and ignorance, reality and illusion, good and evil, life and death. Likewise, he is himself rent by the contradictions of his life: the struggle between his two selves—real and idealized.

He loses emotional and psychological poise when the real self is overpowered by devitalizing forces. R. D. Laing discusses at some length the phenomenon of psychotic alienation when a person can have mystical or magical experiences. "When the 'self' becomes more and more a participant in phantasy relationships, less and less a direct participant in real relationships, in doing so it loses its own reality."[14] The convergence of mother and *Kali* image in his mind is symptomatic of his unconscious. Joseph Campbell, in his work, *The Hero with a Thousand Faces*, points out that mythological and legendary heroes have psychological significance for modern man. The works of psycho-analysts like Freud, Jung and others have found the patterns and logic of myths and dreams correlating. It is "symbolic expression . . . given to the unconscious drives, fears and tensions that underlie the conscious part of human behaviour."[15] In a normal and self-actualizing person his manifestation could have brought the vital psychic energies into action to lend a mature comprehension of the world. In Nirode, it is just a neurotic projection.

To comprehend the overall behaviour of Nirode and to gauge his disturbed state of mind, we have to explore the psychological terrain of his inner being. Nirode's problem, some readers argue, arise out of his Oedipus complex. Like Hamlet, he hates his mother for her supposed relations with the detestable Major Chadha. References to his childhood period disclose Nirode's adoration for his mother. As a grown-up, he hates her—the "she-cannibal," the "cobra" who swallowed his father. His words show his shocking disregard of filial piety. One cannot, however, say that Nirode's hate is sexual in nature. Third Fore psychologists do not align Oedipus complex to libidinal urge as Freudians do. Erich Fromm, in his work *Psychoanalysis and Religion* (1950) transfers it from the sphere of sex to that of impersonal relations. He points out that the child's incest wish is not sexual craving but a desire for security, the urge to remain protected. Horney also believes that mother or father-obsession arises out of environmental situation. In order to compensate for the hostile environment at home, a child clings to one of the parents. Nirode, as we have seen earlier, is attached to his mother. She is a doting mother and fulfils his need for affection. However, after their father's death he notices her bias in favour of Major Chadha. His reaction is intense, not only because he loses his share of love but his mother's behaviour shakes his cultural identity.

When we explore the psycho-social matrix of the Hindu inner world, we understand full well Nirode's rage. Erik H. Erikson reminds us that identity is expressed in the core of the individual as well as that of a communal culture: "A mature psycho-social identity presupposes a community of people whose traditional values become significant to the growing person."[16] Nirode is born and brought up in the Hindu culture of Bengal. The cult of *Durga*, *Shakti* and *Kali* govern the psychic development of the child. He learns that the mother goddesses are the reservoir of both constructive and destructive energy. His emotional strength resides in his mother. He develops, what psychologists call, maternal feminine identity. As he grows up, the biological factor of his maleness overpowers him. As a young man he identifies himself with his father, thus ascertaining his masculine identity. This is evident from his dream wherein he sees "a nicotine-tinged hand" protecting him from the wild wind. Nirode may have despised his father, yet in the unconscious he is still a protective figure. He dreams of himself being on the wrong side of the barbed wire fence with his father while the mother is on the other side of the "brilliant territory." This identification has further, deeper implications in his unconscious fear that she has killed his father and will kill him, too.

Culturally, his mother's behaviour violates Nirode's moral and social standards. Womanhood in India is deified, particularly motherhood. In one of his lectures, Swami Vivekanand observed to his Western audience that in India woman is mother. Dr. S. Radhakrishnan observes that the Hindu view of woman is an exalted one. She has been assigned the most important function of bearing and rearing children and is seen capable of great heights of self-control and self-denial. With such a sublime picture of motherhood as its backdrop, Nirode cannot digest the loose conduct of his mother. It arouses severe repugnance in him and heightens his alienation. Devoid of her reassuring and confirming touch, he experiences extreme loneliness and separation. He feels an outcast in the world where he was already feeling unwanted. He is seized with violent rage. He feels his home to order his life until every vestige of spontaneity and passion is dregged off. But, he is defeated in it. Finally, when mother rejects him, the fear of losing her affection forever horrifies him. In the intensity of his grief and the alienation of his situation, he considers his father's death and Monisha's death, a foreboding of an impending disaster for him. He is cut off from his former life, sensing the primacy of the non-human. He loses faith in love, life, and turns hysteric: "Amla, I know her now. She is *Kali*, the goddess and the demon are one." (*VC*, p. 263)

A psychological evaluation of Nirode's character scores the fact that he is a representative of the sickness of contemporary existence which fails to give a unified sense of experience to the artist. In fact, Nirode is a social and psychological portrait of one of the most common effects of anxiety-neurosis. It is felt that he is trapped in an existential predicament and there is no rational solution to his problems. But his trouble is not the product of the poignant human condition; it is the result of his sickness, his disintegrated personality. Mother's rejection in the end only serves to heighten his neurotic anxiety and speed up his self-alienation. Enslavement to his glorified self-image, and the inability to transcend the limitations of the solipsistic nightmare, exercise a dehumanizing effect on him.

## II

Nanda Kaul in *Fire on the Mountain* is an old woman caught in the web of what Martin Buber calls, "self-contradictions," "the failure to work out and realise the in-born Thou and what meets it."[17] Nanda Kaul is not aware of the split in her personality caused by the desire of the self to recoil from all contact and yet attempt to reach out to the other. She vascillates between two contradictory forces: withdrawal and involvement, detachment and attachment, "the need to withdraw in order to preserve one's wholeness and sanity and the need to be involved in the painful process of life." Nanda, the oldest of Anita Desai's protagonists, and Raka, the youngest character discussed so far, take recourse to self-destructive isolation as an alternative to their conflicts. While the older woman has a tendency to look back and regret, the younger one is terrified of past, present and future, striving to shut out the agony of experiences.

Both Nanda Kaul and Raka offer the pattern of self-alienation of the severe kind, leading them towards neuroses. Metaphysically, they point to the futility of human existence, the inevitability of human suffering. Raka and Nanda suggest a sickness of soul which is imposed upon them from inside. Outer forces do affect the workings of their minds, but their trouble is ingrained in the sense of insecurity developed in the claustrophobic atmosphere they live in. Raka's predicament is identified in her confrontation with the sordid reality of her home: the "harsh filthy abuse" her mother is subjected to and her pathetic condition. Raka feels as if mother is "wet jelly . . . squelching and quivering," under her feet. (*FOM*, p. 72) Nanda's difficulties arise out of her intense self-contempt generated from her dismal failure in life.

We meet Nanda Kaul at Carignano when she has lived her full life-span. Hers has been an existence choked with activities —the multiple responsibilities of running a household, looking after a brood of children (how many ?, she has lost count of them), and maintaining the social status of her Vice-Chancellor husband. After such a hectic life, with all the mundane responsibilities discharged, a wish for a quiet spell of aloneness and contemplation is understandable. Moreover, the concept is not alien to the Hindu mind. A healthy inwardness awakens in man a yearning for self-communion during which he can hear the voice of the spirit and come close to reality. Dr. S. Radhakrishnan regards silent communion as an essential part of worship: "In every one of us is a secret shrine where no one could intrude, to which we must retire as often as possible and discover what our true self is as distinct from the appearance we present to the world outside."[18] However, Nanda Kaul does not look for peace in Kasauli. She likes the emptiness of Carignano, and enjoys the "starkness" of the town. *The Pillow Book of Sei Shonagon* contains a passage befitting her mental state. When a woman lives alone, her house should wear a look of barrenness. It should be unkempt and shabby:

> extremely dilapidated, the mud wall should be falling to pieces, and if there is a pond, it should be overgrown with water plants. It is not essential that the garden be covered with sage-brush, but weeds should be growing through the sand in patches, for this gives the place a poignantly desolate look. (*FOM*, p. 27)

The novel incorporates a bizarre psychology. In her frustration Nanda frantically searches for detachment. Life has not honoured her claims. As her original self-effacing solution has not worked throughout her life, she substitutes it with the strategy of resignation.

So much is made of the protagonist's rebelliously detached attitude and her desire to live in complete isolation that we tend to regard Nanda Kaul as a formidable old woman who has snapped all ties and discarded every one. It is hard to believe that Nanda is basically a compliant character for whom love is the most desired sentiment, above everything else. Whatever little we learn of her life with her Vice-Chancellor husband is sufficient to analyse her fundamental demands. Her flashbacks on her over-busy days reveal that Nanda strikes a "bargain with fate," which Horney terms as a "deal." As a compliant individual, valuing love as the most essential part of life, she is sure that if she is good and dutiful, others will treat her with love. But the realities of life give her a raw deal. Her husband's infidelity, his utter disregard, the callous attitude of her children deal her blows. The reality of life is: she is not the queen of his home, just an unloved woman, mother of his children, a social symbol of his respectability. Under these circumstances, the choice for Nanda is limited—to fight it or bear it mutely. She chooses the second alternative. Also to save her from self-berating, she quickly builds around her a citadel of self-glorifying virtues. Quietly, she engages herself in the discharge of her family duties.

Nanda does not rave or rant as Maya does in *Cry, the Peacock*. Although both these protagonists are compliant, they differ in their sub-types. Maya is a morbidly dependent woman.

Her strategy demands unquestioned love from others. Anything less than her expectations in love, whether real or imaginary, is retaliated with vindictiveness. Nanda Kaul, on the contrary, is a. self-effacing type. Persons belonging to this category place curbs "on all that is presumptuous, selfish, and aggressive." (*NHG*, p.219) Nanda cripples her capacity to fight, to demand her rights, to be self-assertive. In this "shrinking process," she loses even a normal self-esteem. Psychologists point out that positive self-respect is a basic human need, essential for optimal human health. Every human being has a self which includes an awareness of being human individual, capable of making choices that affect one's life and that of others. This loss is substituted by a glorified self-image. Somewhere in her unconscious, Nanda is an epitome of devotion, duty and sacrifice. Her life pattern amply illustrates it—attending to guests, looking after "so many children," serving her husband efficiently:

> Too many trays of tea would have to be made and carried to her husband's study, to her mother-in-law's bedroom, to the verandah that was the gathering-place for all, at all times of the day. Too many meals, too many dishes on the table, too much to wash up after. (*FOM*, p. 29)

She is ever engaged in her duties disavowing her pride. Hardly ever resentful, she is at the most vexed when guests pour in leaving no privacy.

This is the portrait of a silent sufferer, a martyr, a "subdued victimized self." Nanda is not only helpless in the face of her circumstances but also rendered weak and unassuming by her self-effacing drives. Her husband is too immersed in his affairs with Miss David to notice the self-sacrificing devotion of his wife. The novelist portrays her defencelessness, in the imagery of the lapwing. Nanda thinks of the bird as "nervous and agitated." It is a "hunted, fearful bird, distracted and disturbing." (*FOM*, p. 26) Symbolically, she is like the bird, disturbed, agitated, unable to fight and defend herself. Consciously she thinks of herself as a "night cat" prowling in the dark, but unconscious forces tell her that she is like the bird flying unevenly "through the funeral moonlight." This image flashes across her mind when her husband leaves her alone to carry on his love-affair. To relieve the tension of the situation, she considers her aloneness as "a moment of private triumph, cold and proud." (*FOM*, p. 26)

Indeed, Nanda is neither triumphant, nor proud of her aloneness. She is bitter. Only in order to hide the inner fear of isolation she creates a facade of pride and victory. Her visitors—mostly wives and daughters of lecturers and professors —admire her house-keeping skills. They call her "splendid . . . like a queen." Nanda despises these flatterers, knowing well her predicament, "her eyes had flashed when she heard, like a pair a black blades, wanting to cut them, despising them, crawling grey bugs about her fastidious feet." (*FOM*, p. 18) If Nanda were really proud of her life of withdrawal, she would not have wallowed in self-pity. Throughout the narrative, the refrain is: "Discharge me. . . . I've discharged all my duties. Discharge." Her utterances have a note of compunction. A woman who has carried out her responsibilities towards her husband and settled her children in a spirit of self-sacrifice, has a sense of satisfaction. This contains a joy of creativity, not the tinge of remorse. The inner urge of human life is to create, to generate, to make alive, to bring forth something new out of the hidden treasure of being. Nanda on the contrary derives a weird sense of happiness, of a release from bondage, when the responsibilities are over.

It is to be remembered that Nanda Kaul has nothing to look forward to. Her children are alienated from her. Her misery is implicit in the last sentences she utters before her death. "And her children—the children were all alien to her nature. She neither understood nor loved them. She did not live here alone by choice—she lived here alone because that was what she was forced to do, reduced to doing." (*FOM*, p. 145) Obviously, the children do not care for her. She is a forsaken woman. The novel does not expound the behaviour of her other children but Asha's case suggests that Nanda has failed in her human relations, and has generated difficulties by her compulsive drives. Asha is her least-loved daughter, as Nanda recollects. She has been "the most exasperating of her daughters," (*FOM*, p. 14) who compensates for the lack of love in her life by dedicating her entire life-time to beautifying herself. Later, when she is a mother, she neglects Tara, her daughter, who grows up a weakling. Tara is ill-treated by her husband, and is totally incapable of fending for herself. Tara's daughter, Raka, pays for the sins of her parents—father's brutality, mother's nervous breakdown. The graph is clear: Nanda's compulsive drives and her inability to pattern her life, affect three generations.

The dismal sense of having failed at everything in life produces self-reproach and self-contempt. These, in themselves, are damaging feelings. In order to escape the all-consuming self-hate, Nanda must find out some ways. The easiest course open to her is to shift her energies from compliant drives to resignation. As the novel opens, we meet Nanda Kaul, pacing alone the heights of Carignano. A wishless person, she has done with "bags and letters, messages and demands, requests, promises and queries. . . ." (*FOM*, p. 3) We also learn that "it was the place, and the time of life, that she had wanted and prepared for all her life. . . ." (*FOM*, p. 3) She appears to be a resigned individual, all set in for spiritual experience of inner peace. However we soon learn that this is only a semblance of peace, created to run away from conflicts. She feels secure at Kasauli because it is away from the plains where the drama of her life was enacted. Carignano has no memories of her past. Just as Carignano's chequered history is of no relevance to Nanda, so is Nanda's own past to it. An atmosphere of impersonal relations suits her. She has achieved the desired loneliness and feels happy. She has, however, overlooked the basic principle that the past cannot be shut out by fleeing it. As Emerson argues, we can never go out of ourselves. We always perceive our own thought: "It is easy in the world to live after the world's opinion; it is easy in solitude to live after your own; but the great man is he who in the midst of the crowd keeps with perfect sweetness the independence of solitude."[19] Nanda has not achieved the capacity to be timeless and selfless, in the sense Emerson visualises it. Without attaining the optimum liberation of the self, any move in the direction of withdrawal leads to chaos. Nanda confronts her past in Ila and Raka, and is ensnared in her memories.

Nanda Kaul bitterly resents Raka's intrusion because it awakens past memories. She is one of the links of the long chain of events Nanda wishes to forget. So is Ila Das whom she avoids. Both Raka and Ila represent that identity which Nanda strives to forego. Her constant effort is to become anonymous, faceless, to "merge with the pine trees and be mistaken for one. To be a tree, no more and no less, was all she was prepared to undertake." (*FOM*, p. 4) At another time, her desire is to lie still, to "be a charred tree trunk in the forest, a broken pillar of marble in the desert, a lizard on a stone wall. A tree trunk could not harbour irritation, nor a pillar annoyance. She would irritate death, like a lizard." (*FOM*, p. 23) This death-wish shows that she does not want to undergo the past torture again. Once the old connections, binding her to a particular identity in time have been severed, she is sure to feel whole. Raka's arrival breaks her dreams of peace. It is nauseating to follow the same old routine—looking after a child, shouldering responsibility. This will also entail forsaking her newly-acquired freedom. The repetition of what she has done fruitlessly all her life, is unsavoury. Raka's arrival does not elicit an affectionate response. No tangible bond of tenderness develops between them. It is quite unlike the reaction one would expect from a great grandmother.

No affection grows between Raka and Nanda as their solutions of withdrawal clash. Both guard their respective freedoms. At times Nanda's self-effacing trends rise to the surface. She wants to love Raka, yet the child shuns all tenderness viciously. Raka carelessly crushes the newly sprung pink zephyranthes under pebbles and gravels. Her action represents her wish to no longer continue that tenderness which sprung up, like the lilies, between herself and her great grandmother. Children of her age are often attracted towards the beauties of existence: fairy tales, adventure stories, flowers, butterflies and the like. Raka, on the contrary, relates to ugliness. She possesses a weird imagination and is drawn to uncanny places and things. She is not a normal child. Her granny's imaginatively-spun stories can hold her interest for a short while. The bizzare spots of Kasauli, the charred house and trees have an immense fascination for her. Her frequent haunts are the ravines with lizards, snakes, bones and the discarded refuse. No wonder, then, the caretaker of the burnt house thinks of her as "the crazy one from Carignano." (*FOM*, p. 91)

Raka's psychological alienation can be ascribed to her unfortunate home which leaves the child insecure and isolated. If the world is so hostile, the easiest course is to withdraw from it. Instinctively, she learns to expect nothing from it. Conversely, she gives nothing to it. On her part, there is no move to participate in living, to strive for achievement, to socialize. She has lost, what Rollo May calls "intentionality." Intentionality, a preconscious process, gives a person orientation or direction. Impulses—wish, want, will, action, actualization—emerge only after intentionality has made man's experiences meaningful. Loss of intentionality is associated, by psychologists, with schizophrenic disorders and "as such, may derive from early security and relatedness traumata."[20] Rollo May explains this term elaborately as denoting man's capacity to have intentions by which he can mould himself in relation to others. It is a bridge between the subjective and the objective worlds:

> By intentionality, I mean the structure which gives meaning to experience. . . . Intentionality is at the heart of consciousness. I believe that it is also the key to the problem of wish and will. . . .
>
> It is the structure of meaning which makes it possible for us, subjects that we are, to see and understand the outside world, objective as it is. In intentionality the dichotomy between subject and object is partially overcome.[21]

Raka is unable to get in touch with her impulses at the "wish" level and is thus handicapped in finding the deeper roots of her own thrust into life.

Raka's false self sees herself as an independent person, above all socialization and competitions. She resents any attempt to intrude into her ivory tower of privacy. Says the novelist: "Raka had all the jealous, guarded instincts of an explorer, a discoverer. . . ." (*FOM*, p. 61) She hates her great grandmother watching her. In her imagination, she is superior to all, "higher than the eagles, higher than Kasauli and Sanawar and all the other hills." (*FOM*, p. 61) Nanda often compares her own withdrawal with that of Raka and finds that the child is a recluse by nature. This fascinates Nanda. She is once again drawn adrift by her self-effacing love.

Maternal love and her basic nature weaken Nanda's self-imposed detachment. Once again she looks for someone to care for. Her inner dictates force her "to reach out to other," to love and be loved. Horney, in this regard, mentions a compliant person's craving to "strengthen his inner position by being-accepted, approved of, needed, wanted, liked, loved, appreciated." (*NHG*, p. 226) Nanda is filled with tenderness for Raka. Instinctively, she wants to help the child in going to bed and tuck her in. "Habit would rear its head inside her, make her prepare to follow, tell her to tuck the child in, read her a story and lead her safely into sleep." (*FOM*, p. 80) Albeit, Nanda avoids this fresh experience of past enslavement. She experiences a conflict between her compliant and resigned drives. These tendencies pull her in opposite directions: she must keep a safe emotional distance, yet she cannot help being drawn to Raka. Her attitude of resignation warns her that she must avoid any entanglement as she has "suffered from the nimiety, the disorder, the fluctuating and unpredictable excess." (*FOM*, p. 30)

Nanda Kaul is attracted to Raka by the child's natural instinct to reject, to maintain an attitude of careless disregard for company. She notices that Raka has the gift of avoiding what she considers dispensable. She is a child who does not care for love, she "preferred to stand apart and go off and disappear to being loved, cared for and made the centre of attention." (*FOM*, pp. 79-80) These observations work on Nanda's unconscious, and the wish to win Raka's confidence figures therein. All her life, Nanda has tried hard to feel wanted and loved. Consciously and unconsciously, her efforts have been to get a positive response from her family for her devotion, but, all in vain. Now she directs all her energies to hold Raka's interest. She longs desperately for love and realises that if she is discarded, she will be crushed by her self-hate.

The need to reclaim Raka's love indicates Nanda's unconscious longing to feel loved. She weaves around herself a fantasy world. Deriving material from *The Travels of Marco Polo*, substantiating it with imagination, she spins fantastic stories for Raka. It is important to note that her stories are not impersonal accounts of adventure; she gives them a personal appeal with the background of her own maiden home in each one of them. She is gratified when Raka listens with rapt attention. This gives a meaning to her efforts. She makes further attempts to establish a better rapport, which is obvious in the Monkey-point adventure. Nanda Kaul is acting contrary to her initial portrait of an aloof and detached old woman. This is due to her primary self-effacing solution. Withdrawal is the secondary strategy of her defence-mechanism. When the compliant urge comes to the forefront, her forbidding indifference reverts to the background. That is why Nanda once again gets involved in life. She muses on the possibility of bequeathing Carignano to Raka. In one of her last utterances before death she admits that her fabricated stories have had tranquillizing effect on her. "All those graces and glories with which she had tried to captivate Raka were only a fabrication: they helped her to sleep at night, they were tranquillizers, pills." (*FOM*, p. 145) Psychologists agree that daydreams and fantasies are important for human psyche; they represent wish-fulfilment and stand for symbolic satisfaction. The relevance of fantasy in Nanda's case is from a different angle. Raka's interest in her stories gratifies her desire for care and attention from others. She escapes, temporarily though, the remorse and despair of her abject life. It soothes her self-loathing.

So far, Nanda manages to avoid the onslaught of self-hate by escaping alternately into the intra-psychic defences. Finally, the telephone call, announcing the death of Ila Das, overwhelms her with spite for herself. Metaphysically, the deaths of Ila and Nanda are interpreted as the final reality suggesting the futility of human existence: Ila dies because of her concern for others, Nanda dies because of her concern for her loneliness. Both involvement and non-involvement signify a tragic sense of unfulfilment. Feminist criticism spots out a social reality in their deaths, signifying the social forces which destroy women from within. Anita Desai, however, does not subscribe to the view and resents being labelled as a feminist. In reply to an unpublished questionnaire of the present researcher she categorically states that she writes about "the *Human* condition—*Not* the male/female condition." From psychological standpoint we analyse the forces destroying Nanda as the compulsions of self-destructive drives generated by the torment of a life which has been a failure.

On receiving the news of Ila's death Nanda's self-hate operates in several ways. That she fails to stand up to her glorified image impinges upon her unconscious. She is overwhelmed by feelings of worthlessness and inadequacy. A loving individual as she is, she *should* have thought of asking Ila to stay on at Carignano. Self-reproach proclaims her guilty; she is lowered in her self-esteem.

All her life, Nanda lives in pretences. They are, by far, too many—she is the mistress of a happy family; she is always in the hubbub of a busy social whirl; she is the queen of the Vice-Chancellor's house. These pretexts continue and stretch into her old age. She lives in a make-believe world to compensate for the cruel reality. As Tennessee Williams puts it, "There are no lies but the lies that are stuffed in the mouth by the hard-knuckled hand of need, the cold, iron fist of necessity."[22] Each sentence Nanda speaks breaks open the layers of lies she has lived. She sees the reality of her existence; and we realise that she is, in actuality, a woman unloved and discarded. A brief moment of self-scrutiny allows her a glimpse of her lovelessness and misery. Anthony Storr describes a schizoid person as cold, aloof and detached, and calls it "a complex mask for a repressed longing for love,"[23] which may erupt in violent aggression. Although Nanda is not a schizoid case, she has neurotic compulsions

In the end, Nanda Kaul's aggression is directed against her "self" because she has to cope with the struggle between her idealized and real selves. In her last moments we discern that behind the fragmented world reflected by her self-accusations, lies the vision of reality; a brief interplay of life and death, destruction and renewal, chaos and cosmos. Finally, the negative values, chaos and destruction, overpower her real self which a lifetime of pretences has already enfeebled. An inevitable by-product of the confrontation between real and idealized selves is inner conflict. Nanda condemns herself as a murderer of Ila. Self-destructive drives work on her silently but fatally. She does not commit suicide like Maya or Monisha, nor do her neurotic impulses drive her to violent outbursts like Nirode. Her death-wish, expressed in the preceding pages works on her psyche. It finally causes her psychic death, followed by a sudden physical demise.

The silent self-annihilation of Nanda is immediately followed by a more violently destructive act of Raka. Setting the hill-side to fire shows the girl's pyromania. Psychoanalysts consider fire "the objective phenomenon of an inner rage, of a hand which has become irritable."[24] Stealing fire is known as Prometheus complex, signifying disobedience. The destructiveness of Raka's action is sadistic in Horneyan terminology. Horney takes sadism out of its sexual connotation and fits it into a larger theory of human nature. According to her, sadism is ultimately rooted in one's helplessness. She remarks: "Nobody develops pronounced sadistic trends who has not a profound feeling of futility as regards his own life." This arises out of the unconscious realization of a gap between the self and his falsely elaborated view of himself. Raka lessens her conflicts by violence. This is an avenue of escape. By an act of setting fire to the hill-side she saves her ideal self from annihilation. This is an externalization of self-loathing.

Nanda's apparent bellicosity and rebellious detachment are so balanced with the defencelessness of Ila, in the novel, that the latter appears pale by contrast. Ila, reduced to abject poverty—material, personal and social—is, by far, a pathetic figure. Helpless and destitute, she evokes our pity. Whereas behind Nanda's weary detachment lies strong self-effacing urges, behind Ila's powerlessness and ineffectuality is an intense love for power, the urge to master life. Ila Das has seen many vicissitudes of life. There was a time when the family could afford "honey for tea," piano lessons, badminton and other luxuries of the anglicized rich classes of India. Grilled by fate, she seems to understand life. She observes to Nanda, "we must do the best we can. . . . We must simply shoulder our responsibilities and do what we can." (*FOM*, p. 132) Nevertheless, these words of wisdom are not the spontaneous expressions of an affirmation of life. In fact, Ila overacts to surmount her insecurity and loneliness. She attempts to sound least self-conscious and conjure up only a beautiful picture of her painful existence, so as to save herself from despair. It is a refuge. Among the expansive type she falls under the category of the perfectionist people. Ila identifies herself with her high standards and fulfils her obligations well. She imposes the same standards upon the villagers and brings about her end.

In sum, the three female characters in the novel choose their own value systems to guard themselves from reality. Raka refuses to relate herself to the world and regales in being ruined: "I'm shipwrecked and alone. She clung to a rock—my boat, alone in my boat on the sea. . . ." (*FOM*, pp. 61-62) Ila Das claims invulnerability by endowing herself with superiority even in her loneliness. She says to Nanda Kaul: "I am always alone. I am never afraid." (*FOM*, p. 138) Nanda Kaul has a small spell of self-discovery, but the truth about herself is too bitter to endure.

## NOTES

1. D.S. Maini, "Anita Desai's Novels: An Evaluation," in *Perspectives on Anita Desai*, p. 24.
2. Bernard J. Paris, *A Psychological Approach to Fiction*, p. 42.
3. Caroll Davis, *Room to Grow* (London: University of London Press, 1967), p. 3.
4. W.H. White, *The Autobiography of Mark Rutherford* (1881; rpt. London: Fisher, Unwin, 1903), p. 76.
5. D.H. Lawrence, *Phoenix: The Posthumous Papers of D.H. Lawrence*, ed. McDonald (New York: Viking Press, 1936), p. 390.

6. Rollo May, *Love and Will* (New York: Norton, 1969), p. 211.
7. Aldous Huxley, *Island* (Harmondsworth: Penguin, 1962), p. 296.
8. Martin Buber, *I and Thou*, trans. Ronald Gregor Smith (New York: Scribner's, 1937) Extract in *Reality, Man and Existence: Essential Works of Existentialism*, ed. H.J. Blackham (New York: Bantam Books, 1965), p. 217.
9. Erik H. Erikson, "Reflections on Ethics and War," *The Yale Review*, 73 (Summer, 1934), pp. 481-86.
10. R.D. Laing, *The Divided Self*, p. 43.
11. S. Radhakrishnan, *Basic Writings*, p. 57.
12. J. Krishnamurthy, *Beyond Violence*, p. 95.
13. *A Psychological Approach to Fiction*, p. 202.
14. Laing, p 141.
15. Joseph Campbell, *The Hero With a Thousand Faces* (1949; rpt. Princeton: Princeton University Press, 1973), p. 256.
16. Erik H. Erikson, "The Concept of Identity in Race Relations," *Daedalus* (Winter, 1966), pp. 145-71.
17. Martin Buber, *I and Thou*, p. 218.
18. *Basic Writings*, p. 56
19. R.W. Emerson, "Self-Reliance" (1841), *Essays and English Traits*, V (1937; rpt. New York: P.F. Collier, 1961), p. 64.
20. James F.T. Bugental, "The Far Side of Despair," in *Humanistic Psychology: New Frontiers*, ed. Dorothy D. Neville (New York: Gardner Pero, 1977), p. 143.
21. *Love and Will*, pp. 223-24.
22. Tennessee Williams, *27 Wagons Full of Cotton and Other Plays* (New York: New Directions, 1953), p. 71.
23. Anthony Storr, *Human Aggression* (New York: Atheneum, 1968), p. 85.
24. Gaston Bachelard, *The Psychoanalysis of Fire*, trans. Alan C.M. Ross (London: Routledge and Kegan Paul, 1964), p. 36.

# 5

# THE FAR SIDE OF DESPAIR

Self-discovery of Nanda, though apparently brief and ineffectual, is bequeathed to Sita in *Where Shall We Go This Summer ?*, in a more rewarding way. After much struggle she realises that there are no values outside life and that an autonomous self can evolve only when the self flows out to the world in an act of participation. Amla and Sarah too are heirs to this affirmative vision of the author, in *Voices in the City* and *Bye-Bye, Blackbird*, respectively.

Sita, Sarah and Amla, though high-strung, introverts, and highly complex, tend to reconcile with life and its problems. This naturally saves them from psychic disaster faced by earlier characters. Sita rises out of her frustrations, dejection and despair by reclaiming her power to "connect," in the Forsterian sense. Sarah's withdrawal, at social and psychological levels, breeds conflicts which she overcomes when she successfully relates herself to the realities of her life with an Indian husband. Amla reaches an awareness of her growth-potential through the intensity of life's experiences. There is, indeed, a specific push in these characters, to seek answers to the pain of existence.

Nevertheless, their reconciliation does not mean any move towards realisation, it does not mean self-actualization, nor does it indicate inner liberation. Yet, their changed perspective is a clear shift from compulsive constrictive drives to healthy and satisfactory existence.

I

*Where Shall We Go This Summer ?* describes Sita's predicament: she stands up to say "No" to the dull tedium of a meaningless existence and ends up by realizing that "yes" is the sensible word to accept, face and live life. The novel, structurally divided into three parts, narrates the story of Sita, its middle-aged heroine. She resents her fifth pregnancy. In order not to give birth to her child by revoking the magic, she goes to Manori, her maiden home. Her stay on the island awakens her to life's reality, and she chooses to accept the routine of her existence. Sita's mental, moral and emotional issues oscillate between the two polarities of Yes and No. As a critic observes, the novel "dramatises two kinds of courage: a struggle between the positive No and a potent Yes "[1] Sita, at a later stage, tells her husband, Raman, that she did not desert them. "No, no—desertion, that's cowardly. I wasn't doing anything cowardly. . . . I was saying No—but positively, *positively* saying No. There must be some who say No, Raman !" (*WSGS*, pp. 148-49) Albeit afflicted by a torpor brought on by the fifth pregnancy, she acts neurotically. Her wish—to hold back the birth by magic—is an outcome of a sick mind. In this she seems to be nearer Maya and Monisha. With her paranoiac rage, enigmatic demands and querulous behaviour she makes her family miserable. The insane obstinacy of her wish to hold back the child, and the overwhelming despair put her in the category of the earlier Desai characters, heading for a neurosis, psychosis or sudden end. But her final resolution to reconcile with life, saves her from a melodramatically drastic end. The "quiet note" with which the novel ends, speaks of the maturity of perception achieved by both Sita and her creator. Anita Desai, in her interview observes that in order to survive in the world, one has to compromise with life:

> Of course if one is alive, in this world, one cannot survive without compromise—drawing the line means certain death, and in the end, Sita opts for life—with compromise—consoling herself with Lawrence's verse, with the thought that she is compelled to make this tragic choice because she is a part of the earth, of life, and can no more reject it than the slumbrous egg can or the heifer or the grain.[3]

This compromise with life is gained after a prolonged period of intra-psychic conflicts. Sita shifts from compliance to rebellion and then to withdrawal, again coming back to compliance. Since she vascillates between her changing strategies, her behaviour is inconsistent and leaves much scope for disparity between her thinking and actions. In the first part of the novel, entitled "Monsoon 67," she rebels against her family and decides to go to Manori, "What I'm doing is trying to escape from the madness *here*, escape to a place where it might be possible to be sane again." (*WSGS*, p. 35) In the vehemence and spite of her bellicosity there appears no redemption for her from madness. The second part "Winter 47," depicts Sita's life twenty years back, her life with her father. Here we can see her development as a compliant person. This part enables us to understand her later conflicts. Alternately, her resigned and aggressive trends dominate the third section "Monsoon 67." This is a continuation of Part I. Raman visits the island to fetch his children. Sita, too, decides to accompany him. Personally, she reconciles with her situation. Socially, she is dubbed "mad" by Moses and his friends. It is to be seen if Sita really achieves a workable solution to her problems or just returns to the same end from where she started.

Consideration of Sita's unusual childhood is necessary to arrive at a proper evaluation of her character. A motherless child, she experiences partially, neglect and uncertainties right through her childhood. Her situation is just the reverse of Maya's in *Cry, the Peacock*. If Maya's father is over-protective who creates a conflicting situation, Sita's father neglects her completely. He has no time for his children. A public figure, admired and revered by the people, he is too far-off and formidable a person for Sita to approach with filial affection.

There is always an "impossibility of talk between her and her father." (*WSGS*, p. 79) He is immersed in his self-glorification and he regards Jivan and Sita just as he considers his sycophant *chelas* and devotees. But, he certainly loves Rekha, his eldest daughter. The atmosphere in which Sita lives and grows is that of neglect, hypocrisy and partiality. Consciously as well as unconsciously, she is uneasy. She questions herself: why and how is it that there is no resemblance between the two sisters ? The disclosure that Rekha is not her real sister drops on her "skin like acid and she felt them burn whenever she caught an exchange of that heavy-lidded look between father and daughter, or his arm in its fine white sleeve lie fondly across her round shoulders." (*WSGS*, p. 79) Here is a clear hint of incest. The two cases of parental partiality, one in *Cry, the Peacock* and the other in *Where Shall We Go This Summer ?* are quite dissimilar. In Maya's case, a tender father's harshness towards a rebel brother is an indication that any move towards independence or autonomy is punishable by withdrawal of love. Maya, therefore, clings to her father for fear of antagonizing him. Sita, on the other hand, feels discarded and unwanted when she notices her father's tenderness towards Rekha. This experience breeds feeling of worthlessness, and its consequent strategy is rebelliousness. Sita cannot corroborate her father's dubious ways. It seeps down her psyche as a bad human experience. Her world is peopled with hypocrisy and hypocrites—the islanders, the *chelas*, Deedar, Rekha, and her father. The only sane and innocent voice is that of Sita who has the courage to make her face wry and declare that the well-water is not sweet. Her environment is injurious. It shatters her faith in life and in the goodness of the world. It is "a strange life, an unusual life"; it does not offer her the freedom to acquire unique individuality but lets her "withdraw into the protective chrysalis of childhood for longer than is usual for most." (*WSGS*, p. 63) The disintegration of family, immediately after father's death, testifies the bitter truth that they had nothing substantial to bind them as a family. Rekha does not even stop to shed tears for him and leaves "as though she had waited for and planned for this moment of release from the old man's love." (*WSGS*, p. 99) Jivan disappears a couple of days before the demise as if he had had a foreknowledge of the calamity. Only Sita stays on, to marry Raman, the first man in her life. The family would not have broken so abruptly had there been a sense of belonging.

Belongingness is a subjective feeling in which an individual experiences personal involvement. The most damaging situation for Sita is complete lack of parental matrix. Hypocrisy and partiality apart, her father cannot provide her a home. Her life starts "in the centre of a crowd."

> With calm eyes she had watched the surge and flow of such masses, listened to endless speeches on one subject, *Swaraj*, had her chin chucked, collected, discarded garlands and played with the tinsel till she fell asleep against a bolster and was carried away to someone's house to sleep—always a different someone, it scarcely mattered which one. She belonged, if to anyone, to this whole society that existed at that particular point in history—like a lamb does to its flock—and saw no reason why she should belong to one family alone. (*WSGS*, p. 55)

As Sita does not have a home, she has no feeling of belonging. "Belongingness . . . means a subjective feeling of one's personal involvement to the extent that one feels himself to be an integral and indispensable part of the system."[3] Involvement can be with another person, an idea or a group. Erich Fromm maintains that by uniting himself with other person in the spirit of love and shared work, man can hope to end his alienation. A family is the most important internal group to condition a person's relationship to himself. R.D. Laing considers family to be internalized in each one of us. It is like a flower, with mother as the centre, the children as its petals around it. The most vital link—the mother—is missing in Sita's life. Unknown to her, a deep seed of insecurity is sown in her life.

This leads to an alienation from self. Her vague fears, an abiding sense of dissatisfaction, nausea and mortal dread of taking on responsibility of the new-comer—all point towards the sense of insecurity bred in childhood. A way out of this is the adoption of some psychological prop: she desperately needs someone to belong to. Deedar's son, Raman, is the first and, of course, the only person to take her out of the shocking isolation after her father's death. Raman gives her the desired security—social as well as psychological. Naturally, Sita leans on him, unconsciously looking up to him as her messiah. She leaves the island with some relief, "Worn out by the drama" of life. Raman appears to her as

> a tired manager drawing the curtains together, locking up the empty theatre. . . . It was as though he had been expressly sent by providence to close the theatrical era of her life, her strange career and lead her out of the ruined theatre into the thin sunlight of the ordinary, the everyday, the empty and the meaningless. (*WSGS*, p. 100)

Sita has been playing a role to guard herself from the crushing circumstances. The need for affection, suppressed so far, raises its head. She is a helpless, lonely young woman, in need of support, and Raman can fulfil the need.

With this unconscious desire in the background, Sita makes a "bargain with fate"—if she is helpless, good and humble, she will be lovable; Raman will love her. As a self-effacing person she poses to be good, without pride, and hopes that she will be treated well by fate and by others. We have the first inkling of Sita's bargain when she submits to the marriage proposal of Raman, who marries her "out of pity, out of lust, out of a sudden will for adventure, and because it was inevitable." (*WSGS*, p. 99) She admits that she bore four children "with pride, with pleasure—sensual, emotional, Freudian, every kind of pleasure. . . ." (*WSGS*, p. 31) Sita builds up a relationship in her mind with her husband, based on the "deal"—she will be an obliging wife; and Raman will honour her self-image for her lovable qualities. For her, love is an engulfing passion, like the vision of the Muslim couple she sees in the Hanging Gardens:

> They were like a work of art—so apart from the rest of us. They were not like us—they were inhuman, divine. So strange—that love, that sadness, not like anything I've seen

> or known. They were so white, so radiant, they made me see my own life like a shadow, absolutely flat, uncoloured. (*WSGS*, pp. 146-47)

Such a love transcends the limits of the self and human finitude. Suno, in Anita Desai's short story "Studies in the Park," sees the same vision of divine love. The Muslim couple are real human beings belonging to this world but the intensity of their tenderness is beyond human limitations. Suno affirms, "no one else in my life had been real and alive." (*GAT*, p. 31) After these moments of empathy both Sita and Suno find ordinary life unbearably dull and drab. To Suno everything appears purposeless and lifeless compared to this scene. Sita tells Raman that it was the happiest moment of her life. This confession enrages him, though Sita means no offence. As we evaluate her defence-mechanism we discover the working of her glorified self-image. She is like the helpless Muslim woman, needing all attention and tenderness. She expects Raman to be like the lover, making her realise how valuable she is to him. Raman, however, does not honour the claims of her bargain, and the dream is never realised.

Raman has his own compulsions to deal with. He marries Sita out of pity, as we have already discussed earlier. When this initial stage of lust and pity wears off (like Shelley and Harriet Westbrook wedlock), Raman finds his mundane activities more fascinating and fulfilling. He is an expansive person who wants mastery over life. Individuals like him resent those who depend too much because conversely they are scared that such persons may exercise control over them. Raman shifts his energies towards his business so as to escape his intra-psychic and inter-personal conflicts. By nature he is not aggressive but a "perfectionist." He has set his standards and must strictly adhere to them. He is meticulous and punctilious in fulfilling his obligations,—"everything was so clear to him, and simple: life must be continued, and all its business—Menaka's admission to medical college gained, wife led to hospital, new child safely brought forth, the children reared, the factory seen to, a salary earned, a salary spent." (*WSGS*, pp. 138-39) Sita secretly admires him for his courage and endurance. According to Horney, a perfectionist achieves "behavioristic perfection" and he insists upon others "living up to his standards of perfection and despises them for failing to do so." (*NHG*, p. 196) Raman, therefore, cannot tolerate lack of control shown by Sita. He is fair, just and dutiful, so Sita should also be fair to him. He cannot understand her rebelliousness. Their contradictory drives drag them apart, making it difficult for each to comprehend the motives of the other.

Raman's failure to recognise Sita's self-effacing drives and honour her capacity for surrender and love, injures her self-image. Her hopes of getting love are frustrated. She tells him once: "I thought I could live with you and travel alone—mentally, emotionally. But, after that day, that wasn't enough. I had to stay whole, I *had* to." (*WSGS*, p. 148) The concept of staying "whole" requires a little elaboration. Sita, here, does not refer to the idea of individuation or self-realization. She does not bother about self-realization. All she wants is to feel her glorified self. Raman's inability to honour her claims of love, impinges upon her psuedo-self. Her neurotic pride is hurt and she turns vindictive. She must restore her damaged self-esteem: so, she tries to attract attention by being plaintive, and complaining of her unhappiness; secondly, she openly rebels against all social and familial norms in order to feel triumphant.

She rebels against the "vegetable existence" lived by the women of Raman's family—initially, it is only a verbal attack, then she takes recourse to a more flagrant disregard for their way of life by taking to smoking. Shocking them thus, Sita enjoys a sense of superiority. Raman is startled when she describes his business associates as animals: "They are nothing—nothing but appetite and sex. Only food, sex and money matters. Animals." (*WSGS*, p. 47) This outburst vexes Raman who is "not an introvert, nor an extrovert—a middling kind of man . . . dedicated unconsciously to the middle way." (*WSGS*, p. 47) One immediately recalls Maya in *Cry, the Peacock*. Maya shows her disgust for the people and the entire atmosphere at the Lals's party. Gautama is irritated and he exhorts her to learn to bear everyday mediocrity. Sita also baffles Raman by her behaviour and enjoys having thus annoyed him. It gives her a sense of triumph.

Again, Sita enjoys her victory when she often broaches the subject of the hitch-hiker. "She not only thought again and again of that wanderer's mirage-like appearance and disappearance but spoke too often and too much of him." (*WSGS*, p. 52) Raman is amused, astonished and then annoyed. His perfectionist moral standards receive a jolt; his male-ego is hurt. Tension mounts because "he regarded her admiration for, and interest in, the hitch-hiker practically as an act of infidelity." (*WSGS*, p. 53) Sita has no physical attraction for the stranger, but mentally she feels a kinship with him. For some readers this episode contains Sita's quest-urge personified in the wanderer. From psycho-analytical point of view, this shows her hostile-aggressive drive, not only for a vindictive triumph over Raman but also to restore her neurotic pride. This is an attempt at self-preservation.

Sita shows "psychic fragmentation" or compartmentalization which is described in psychiatric literature as a disintegrating process. In it a neurotic fails to see himself as a whole entity and experiences himself in piecemeal, which saves him from conflicts and tensions created by his inner contradictions. The function of compartmentalization is to "preserve the *status quo*, to protect neurotic equilibrium from collapsing." (*NHG*, p. 180) Quite unawares, she experiences herself in fragments. For example, on one hand she cherishes her image of a helpless, suffering woman seeking almost divine love from Raman. On the other hand, she is a rebel feeling one with the aimless wanderer, This inability to view herself in wholeness brings out the contradiction latent in her personality. In E.M. Forster's *Howard's End*, Margaret exhorts Henry Wilcox, "live in fragments no longer." The final reconciliation is achieved in the act of harmonious living and establishing contact with the earth. Sita moves towards "wholeness" only when she discovers the essential cosmic kinship. Her personality regains integration when she recovers the ability to "connect." Forster's words "only connect" remain in her subconscious without making deeper penetration, till then.

Denying herself joy, enthusiasm, anger and fear—the whole range of sentiments that make us human—Sita loses the urge to assert and affirm herself. Devoid of these natural feelings, she becomes a melancholy, depressed woman, bored with life; nothing can instil zeal in her. She presents a gloomy picture to her children and a quizzical one to her husband—sitting on the balcony, smoking endlessly, staring blankly at the sea, as if she were waiting for something. Her entire life acquires the colour of waiting:

> It was not a pure colour—it was tinged at times with anxiety, at others with resignation. Or with frenzy, patience, grimness, fear. But whatever its tint, its tone, it had seeped through her, flowed along every smallest capillary till she herself was turned to the colour of waiting, was turned a living monument of waiting. (*WSGS*, pp. 54-55)

On a deeper level, waiting presupposes the beginning of a wish to reach beyond a state of despair and transcend emptiness and apathy into constructive potentialities. In Sita's case, the vacuity exercised by her neurotic control system, blocks the possibility for assertion and spontaneity. The control imposed upon impulses and feelings is let loose; fear disrupts her mental equilibrium. It may be pointed out, here, that automatic control system is a neurotic measure adopted to relieve the tension of self-alienation; whereas a normal self-control imposed upon unwanted desires and wants is a healthy attribute. The failure of automatic control system produces "fright responses." Sita becomes panicky with her fifth pregnancy.

The terror of the ensuing child-birth that Sita harbours, has several psychological causes. Her confinement will force her to forsake her strenuously guarded strategies of detachment. It will entail getting involved in life once again—physically as well as emotionally. A deeper psychic reason, however, is the fear of her guilt-feeling caused by the awareness that she has not exercised self-control in sexual desires. Self-reproach in the form of a gnawing feeling "I should have known," makes her feel small. Her rage indicates an externalization of the inner turmoil. Says the novelist: "It was as though for seven months she had collected inside her all her resentments, her fears, her rages, and now she flung them outward, flung them from her." (*WSGS*, p. 33)

Sita thus gives vent to her fury in order to protect herself from the onslaught of her self-hate. At the same time, there are visible signs of "self-tormenting intents" working within her psyche. Her desire to keep the child inside her is a kind of procrastination meant to continue her suffering. Since her primary drive is self-effacement, the urge to magnify her suffering is a part of her mental make-up. Horney calls it "Schaden fende" i.e. a vindictive statisfaction at the self-inflicted pain. This is confirmed by Anita Desai's observation in an interview with Jasbir Jain that in Sita's wish to perpetuate her pregnancy there is a kind of "rebellion right through to the last moment." She goes to Manori revolting against all norms and advice. She becomes militantly aggressive towards all—Raman, her children and later towards Moses. This single motif—not to give birth—on which the entire structure of the novel is based, shows the combination of her compounded solutions—withdrawal, expansion and self-effacement. By closing her eyes to the reality and resolutely following her fantasy, Sita manages to make herself immune from the assault of her self-loathing. She wrests a kind of victory by rebelling against her bondage, and overcoming her weakness. In protecting her child from the callous world, Sita is in fact, guarding her self-image.

To the world she appears crazy. Her attitude, her outbursts of anger, her appearance all substantiate her whimsical approach. Is Sita really "mad" as Moses and his friends describe her ? Why is she always angry ? The answer lies in the aggressiveness brewing within her as her self-effacing solution fails. She wants to master life somehow, and by her behaviour she creates an atmosphere denuded of love. Menaka is grown-up enough to retaliate her mother's strange moods by her defiance. The girl comprehends that she can rely more on her father than on her moody mother. Sita is never normal with her children; as such they are attached to Raman. Whatever solution Sita adopts—self-effacing, aggressive or resigned—she is always heavily charged under her own pride system. She either bores them by her perpetual misery, or intimidates them by her arrogant-vindictive drives. Or her detached unconcern keeps them at a distance. Her capacity to give spontaneous love is seriously impaired.

When Sita's compliant and expansive remedies fail, she resorts to withdrawal. We see her mostly bored with and disinterested in life. She neglects her appearance, grows defiant and difficult to approach. A mental and physical inertia pervades her spirit. Her own children mean only "anxiety, concern—pessimism. Not happiness." (*WSGS*, p. 147) She grows an onlooker on life, keen only to guard her freedom. The very idea of leaving the island and going back to Mainland means compromising her freedom. In moments of tension she tells her foetus, "I'll keep you safe inside. We'll go nowhere." (*WSGS*, p. 127)

Sita does not have a healthy man's concept of freedom. Spontaneity is the pre-condition of positive freedom. It overcomes loneliness and insecurity, and helps in affirmation of life. Sita, on the contrary, resorts to the "mechanisms of escape" as Erich Fromm terms it. She attains only freedom from conflicts. The pathological side of her escape is an effort at forgetting the real self because she is desperate to maintain the identity of her glorified self-image. She succeeds in making her life merely a condition of exile, uprooting herself from her setting. Fromm explains it as the "other course" before a man which is not conducive to integrity and self-realization, rather it is an escape from an unbearable situation and is characterized by its compulsive character.

> The other course open to him is to fall back, or to give up his freedom, and to try to overcome his aloneness by eliminating the gap that has arisen between his individual self and the world. . . . It assuages an unbearable anxiety and makes life possible by avoiding panic; yet it does not *solve* the underlying problem and is paid for by a kind of life that often consists only of automatic and compulsive activities.[4]

The compulsive nature of Sita's attitudes discloses itself in her neurotic fear of violence. She becomes panicky at the "small incidents" of life—the boys fighting, Menaka tearing her painting or crushing unawares the tender buds of a potted plant, *Ayah's* brawling. Her strong reactions disturb and astound Raman: "If you are an adult you know how to cope with them—they are only *small* incidents." (*WSGS*, p. 37) A normal individual takes such things as trifles, one comes across in daily life. As we probe deeper we discover that violence terrifies Sita because it is within her. It sounds unbelievable that a person like Sita, who spends long hours in guarding a wounded eaglet, should breed violence. But, it is true. Destructiveness, Fromm believes, is the result of an unlived life. Man has an inner dynamism in him with tendency to grow. If this is thwarted, the dynamic energy decomposes and is directed towards destructiveness. Failure in life makes her vindictive. Her own "fury" and revengefulness frighten her. She is now obviously scared of all outside violence because she fears her inner violent tendencies.

Sita's perception clears only towards the end of the novel. In D.H. Lawrence's verse she finds an answer to her problem. So far she has considered giving birth an act of violence but now she realises that a seed fallen from the tree of life into the cosmic womb, must break open. There can be no life without growth into a full organism. Bursting out of the enclosure of the womb is a violent activity, but in its impetuosity it is creative. In his *Fantasia*, Lawrence maintains that pure passionate destructive activity and pure passionate constructive activity are the same, religiously. Sita realises that "the strange, new knocking of life at her side," is indicative of a flow of energy, which must be released, to fertilize a new life. With this awareness, her self-questioning consciousness, gets busy in the task of self-improvement. This is her moment of inspiration; in it she establishes a contact with her authentic self. Sita achieves integration of her personality by arriving at a fusion with the world. When the self flows out in a spirit of creativity and spontaneity, she grapples with her real self. On the island, in the midst of nature, she experiences oneness with her surroundings. She becomes conscious of "presences"—the presence of the island itself, of the sea around it, and of the palm trees that spoke to each other and sometimes even to her." (*WSGS*, p. 126) She does not feel lonely. Even when the children are away, she feels one with them "considering how much and how close together they were in that isolated house." (*WSGS*, p. 126)

One more experience, small but relatively significant, enables Sita to recognise her sensibilities and prowess as the self in relation to the earth. It occurs when she plays with Karan with an "oblivious joy," all soaked in mud. She loses all self-consciousness and regains childhood innocence. This leads her to a unifying sense of oneness. For Maslow, this denotes freedom from inhibitions, and is one of the paths leading to real self. Sita's move from fragmentation to a cosmic awareness enhances her chance of self-discovery.

Here we see a full fructification of E.M. Forster's phrase "only connect" which remains buried in her consciousness for long. Forster employs it in three different connotations. In *Howards End* it implies the connecting of individuals within themselves to achieve a "wholeness." In *A Passage to India*, it stands for establishing a connection between individual and individual, as well as on the racial and national levels. The push in Sita's psyche, at this stage, is towards developing a harmony in personal relationships and establishing a contact with the earth. The cosmic and personal synthesis, so gained, help her in seeing beyond despair.

All along, Sita is severely depressed, but the saving grace of her situation lies in her not becoming will-less and wishless like Desai's earlier protagonists—Maya, Monisha, Nirode and Nanda. Despair and dejection, the humanistic psychologists tell us, act as warning signals. If we heed them we can check the disintegration of our personality. S. Jourard observes that human system has built-in indicators, like machines, emitting signals when fatigue, frustration or other damaging impulses exceed tolerance. If one hears these cues, he can recover the self:

> Doubtless, when a person is behaving in ways that do violence to the integrity of his system, warning signals are emitted. If only man could recognize them himself, and institute corrective action . . . 'Normal,' self-alienated

> man. however, often ignores his tilt signals—anxiety, guilt, fatigue, boredom, pain or frustration—and continues action aimed at wealth, power or normality until the machine stops.[5]

In Sita, there is a temporary blockage of consciousness, but she shows steady signs of a dynamism for constructiveness. There is no breakdown of her power to wish and will. It helps her in self-direction. The latent urge in her is to be creative. She tells Menaka that if she had the talent to paint or sing she would have nursed it to full growth. Creativity would have lent meaning to her life:

> if only I could paint, or sing, or play the *Sitar* well, really well, I should have grown into a sensible woman. . . . I should have known how to channel my thoughts and feelings, how to put them to use. I should have given my life some shape then, some meaning. (*WSGS*, p. 117)

Conflicts and awareness of conflicts are in themselves a sure sign of relative health. Sita has the capacity to reach out for full humanness.

We cannot say that Sita is a fully self-actualized individual. Only, she has a potential for that. She looks within. There are human limitations. She feels stranded like a jelly-fish, symbolically representing her inner self. In one image Sita sees herself as the jelly-fish; in another, the fish and her foetus become one as the "opaque" brain of a gigantic sea-monster. The fish symbolises the amoeba of life. In recognising the central point of the brain of the sea-monster, she becomes aware of her self. As Jung points out, the central point within the psyche is the core of personality; the source of energy which manifests itself in man's urge to become the "self."

Sita's compromise with life constitutes a sure step forward to recognise reality. The awareness that life is not meant to be shunned but to be experienced, is significant. Participation in the act of living leads to the acceptance of a fuller responsibility. Symbolically, when Sita walks back home placing her feet in Raman's foot-marks on the sand, she decides to contribute positively to *their* lives. Sita's existential *angst* is displayed in her thoughts, "life had no periods, no stretches. It simply swirled around, muddling and confusing, leading nowhere." (*WSGS*, p. 155) Here, her personal problems transcend into existential ones and her neurotic despair and anguish give way to a more philosophic perception of the absurdity of human condition. If human existence is so impoverished, it is better to affirm life, here and now. According to May Sarton, "private dilemmas are, if deeply examined, universal and so if expressed, have human value beyond the private."[9]

At times one finds Sita's affirmation and reconciliation too unassertive, signifying a defeat of individuality. At the end of the novel we cannot tell whether she manages to lead a healthy life after her return to Bombay, or she simply strides back into her former neurotic rages and fears. When asked about the child, Anita Desai affirms in an interview that the child is born and learns to compromise:

> It is born. It lives. It adjusts. It compromises. It accepts dullness, mediocrity, either closes its eyes to or else condones destruction, ugliness, rottenness. In other words, it leads an ordinary life of the kind its mother tried so desperately to change only to find she could not.

The above words convey acceptance; life ceases to be an absurdity and becomes a general fact of the human experience. By implication we infer that it is a tangible expression of an inner change in Sita. Acceptance shows growth, ripeness; it implies the process of actualization. The ability to "connect" the fragments of life and achieve an integration will perhaps enable her to realise her place and experience herself as a part of a larger whole.

## II

Sarah in *Bye-Bye, Blackbird*, is a case of both social and psychological alienation. The social factor stems from her marriage to an Indian settled in England; her psychological trouble emanates from her pride system. The novel is, thus, a departure from Desai's other works in its emphasis upon the cultural factors in shaping the individual psyche. The characters or events do not offer a sociological thesis in her handling of the East-West-encounter theme. Many critics read this novel chiefly as a presentation of the social isolation of Adit and Sarah,"[7] or as a "depiction of racial and cultural problems. Thematically, it is the story of Dev and Adit. These two male characters dominate the field of action, yet it is Sarah who remains the palpitating presence throughout the narrative.

Anita Desai displays her skill of characterization in dealing with the psyche of Sarah. Meenakshi Mukherjee considers Sarah the most successful and a typical Desai character, "complex, hyper-sensitive and intelligent."[8] She can claim kinship with the introverted heroines of *Cry, the Peacock* and *Voices in the City*. The parallelism, however, ends here. Sarah does not suffer from inner vacuity like the earlier two heroines, though she is temporarily alienated. In dealing with the problem of Sarah, stuck with duality and uncertainties, the novelist projects a comprehensive view of the dilemmas of an alienated self. Desai's interpolations of Indian exuberance and British reticence, and her penetrating study of the impact of English literature on Indian intellectuals, forms the whole range of Indo-British experience. Thus, social and psychological realism runs side by side in the narrative.

Fear, insecurity and the resultant withdrawal are the three major motifs of the novel. The novel incorporates the impact of an East-West marriage on the psyche of Sarah. Adit marries Sarah, an English woman, settles in England and feels at home there. Dev reaches England from India for higher studies. He is soon nauseated by the racial prejudices. He is highly critical of everything English. Their attitudes take a sudden turn after their return from a weekend spent in the suburb of London: Dev starts loving England whereas Adit is nauseated. He decides to leave for India. "For the Sens, the weekend ended in a mottled grey fade-out of regret and apprehension as they drove off . . . but for Dev the adventure had only begun." (*BBB*, p. 190) Although the novel revolves round the two male characters, the main story concerns Sarah, who lives in a dual world—the two social worlds that do not meet; the two incompatible cultures that split her.

Disharmony prevails in Sarah's familial life and seems to threaten her marriage. We learn of Adit's tastes. He hates English cooking and Sarah has not learnt to cook Bengali food to his satisfaction. Whereas Sarah does not relish Indian music, Adit loves it. She remains an alien in Adit's social circle not equipped to participate in their jokes, conversations and laughter. It would however, be naive to conclude that these factors create marital dissonance. One feels that Adit and Sarah have adjusted to each other despite these differences. His romantic love for England is matched by the romanticism of her imagination about India. They maintain their cultural identities, yet experience a close affinity with each other's culture. But, Sarah has a dread of being labelled an Indian wherein lies the crux of her difficulty. Her sense of shame and nervousness are so obvious that some readers tend to agree with her colleague, Julia, "If she's that ashamed of having an Indian husband, why did she go and marry him ?" (*BBB*, p. 42) Sarah's irrational fear is not an outcome of her social alienation only. We can analyse her motives in the light of her anxiety behind her psychological upheaval.

Sarah's real anxiety springs from the perfectionist atmosphere of her parental home. Perfectionism identifies itself with its standards. Generally, we consider perfectionism in terms of being punctual, careful and meticulous in matters like conversation, dress and behaviour. But, psychologists regard these as superficial aspects. For them a perfectionist is, as a rule, extra-careful in achieving a "flawless excellence of the whole conduct of life." (*NGH*, p. 196) Horney groups perfectionism as one of the three sub-types under the expansive solution. Sarah is the product of a traditional English home with its set rules and rigid norms. She knows that the atmosphere in British homes in general is of strict regimentation. She tells Dev:

> . . . ninety out of every hundred people here live lives exactly alike. Every evening they watch the same programmes on the telly, every Friday night they go to the local for a pint, every Saturday they have roast beef for lunch, every Witsun and Bank holiday stream down to the sea like lemmings. . . . (*BBB*, p. 146)

The Roscommon-James, Sarah's parents, seem no exception. She remembers her father, now turned an old and awkward gardener, as a sophisticated, well-read and respectable physician, living in Winchester "in a house in which oak panels gleamed and porcelain sparkled." (*BBB*, p. 164) Her mother, though "coarse-grained and clumsy," was a strict mother—rather a Tory matron—who would reprimand Sarah if her skirts were above her knees.

Brought up in this atmosphere of regimentation, Sarah channelises her feelings, to project herself as an obedient girl. It follows, then, that as a loving daughter she *should* love her parents and *accede* to their wishes willingly. As long as she is able to identify with her image, there is no conflict. Her only act of non-conformity, of marrying an Indian, divests her of self-righteousness. Her weakness tickles her pride and she becomes rebellious. Its immediate reaction is that of shame which appears in her consciousness in the form of vague uneasiness. As existentialists observe, shame arises out of our awareness of ourselves on introspection. The recognition of her failure to measure up to her expectations produces in Sarah self-reproach.

Sarah's self-accusation does not interfere with their married life, it is only damaging for her mental health. Although we are not told about her parents's reaction to the wedding, we learn about their resentment by her father's displeasure and mother's unconcealed bitterness towards Indians. Her father changes into a reticent old man from an exhuberant physician. The process of his alienation is triggered, not so much by the country-life as by the jolt to his perfectionist standards. Sarah is intelligent enough to understand this change; she also comprehends her mother's hostility. This creates inter-personal and intra-psychic conflicts in her, threatening disintegration of personality. She can resolve them, so she must escape them to save her self.

Sarah, therefore, takes recourse to withdrawal. Over the years she has learnt the art of "side-stepping." In her own social circle in the school, she finds it easier to let others talk of themselves rather than discuss her life. This is how she minimizes her conflicts. When this privacy is eroded, or demands are made on her, she recoils—as in the case of Philippa

Grodge. Sarah buys a chocolate for the girl but the moment the child queries about Indian postage-stamps, she withholds her gift. Consciously she feels as if the child had let out her secret: "Out it tumbled, rattling, terrible—a nut, a crab, a grain of sand. There it lay—her secret." (*BBB*, p. 38) What is so confidential about Indian stamps when they all know that she is married to an Indian ? Actually, she wishes to guard it not so much from others as from herself that she is making "efforts to know India, become Indian. . . . To have anyone pry upon them, break in upon the shadowed intimacy of her relationship with them, was violent, shaking, terrible." (*BBB*, p. 38)

The strategy of withdrawal is characterized by emotional distance. A detached person recoils from emotional demands made on him. In Sarah's case, it is particularly obvious when she receives her mother's letter advising her to think seriously before leaving for India. Sarah is impatient with the letter. She rejects it callously as if disposing of her mother summarily. Adit finds her cruel. Sarah's reaction is so vehement that she cannot even tolerate being addressed as "Sally" which reminds her of her mother. She snaps at Adit: "Don't call me Sally." She defends herself against all emotional demands by protestations of her individuality:

> Don't *you* treat me the way she always does—as though I'm not an individual with my own life to lead, but just—just some appendage to them, with nothing but duties and responsibilities instead—instead of *rights*. If I were you, I'd be ashamed to listen to that nonsense for one minute. (*BBB*, p. 250)

The force of this outburst surprises us until we understand the conflict in her mind. Sarah is not an assertive individual, but by justifying her annoyance she tries to by-pass her self-accusation. This is a face-saving device. Her assertion that she values her individuality over and above her love for parents, serves to convince her of the exigency of her actions. She, thus, seeks to externalize her self-hate. In other words, she rebels unconsciously because her mother ignored her rights and made her lead a life of regimentation.

Intrinsically, Sarah is a demure and reticent young woman. Adit is impressed by her "shyness and rectitude." He tells her in the early days of their courtship:

> You are like a Bengali girl . . . reserved, quiet. May be you were one in your previous life. But you are improving on it. You are so much prettier. (*BBB*, p. 84)

After wedding, her reticence turns into aloofness. Sarah loses her zest to participate in living: apathy pervades her. She feels empty, and ineffectual in directing her life. Sarah is not lonely, socially. At home, there are Adit, Dev and their social circle. In school, she has her colleagues. But amid the crowd Sarah is solitary: she cannot enjoy the company of her countrymen, nor can she be at home in Adit's social circle. The former is psychological, the latter cultural alienation. She refuses to work out any co-ordination and wants to escape socialization by hiding.

Indeed, Sarah's problem is rooted in her cross-cultural marriage. Her bewilderment and frustration is the result of what Toffler calls "cultural shock." Immersion in a strange culture "causes a breakdown in communication, a misreading of reality, an inability to cope."[9] Sarah is overwhelmed by the change because she cannot fully involve herself in her husband's culture, nor can she adopt herself to her own society. Normally, within our own community, each of us has a unified self. Cultural values give us this specific identity. But under certain pressures, the personality may break up and different selves spring-up. Van den Berge prefers to call it "sociosis"[10] rather than "neurosis" when socio-historical alterations affect the psychology of an individual. Sarah's dual estrangement comes, not from social transformation within her society but from a cross-cultural catalysis of her own choice.

Cross-cultural relations do not always bring in psychological disaster. In Kamala Markandaya's *Some Inner Fury*, for example, Mira and Richard love each other truly and intensely. Although circumstances force Mira to leave Richard and join the procession of Indian patriots, she continues to love him. She reflects on their love as a source of immortal happiness:

> What had been given us had been gifted freely, abundantly, lit with a splendour which had coloured and enriched our whole living; it could never be taken from us. We had known love together, whatever happened the sweetness of that knowledge would always remain. We had drunk deeply of the chalice of happiness, which is not given to many even to hold.[11]

This kind of perfect unison in love is lacking in Sarah-Adit relations. Sarah makes no positive effort "to connect herself" to India. It is a culture she willingly adopts, but with it she cannot assimilate. "Accept acceptance,"[12] Paul Tillich advises modern man, because it is essential for an individual to unify his experiences into a single consistent and coherent personality. Problems arise for Sarah as she finds herself inadequate to her own British society; and for her, Indian culture is insufficient. This is her dual estrangement. To mention India and her Indian husband to her English friends "would have forced her to parade like an imposter, to make claims to a life, an identity that she did not herself feel to be her own." (*BBB*, p. 42)

Sarah vascillates between her two selves—public and private. Her self-image of perfect English vein needs preservation in public. Privately, she does not dislike India or Indians. Once she shuts herself up in the cosy intimacy of her home, she is self-confident, composed and happy. She can also be free with Emma, their aged landlady. She says to Adit: "To have Emma Moffit with her was merely like having a mirror in the room." (*BBB*, p. 45) This observation shocks him because there is apparently no resemblance between the two. Emma's obsession with India, where her English fiance had died long back, has a distinctly eccentric quality of its own than Sarah's shy concern for India and Indians. She believes that if Adit had not married her or if he were to desert her, she might become an eccentric like Emma. These are not light-hearted passing remarks, meant to tease her husband. They display her sense of insecurity.

Adit chides Sarah for imagining such things and calls her an "icicle." She is not altogether an "icicle", though she loses the warmth of her personality in an effort to connect her two selves. Her problems become acute as her relations to herself turn impersonal. Ashamed of herself, she moves away from her real self. This alienation is suggested through dream. During their weekend visit to Sarah's parents, she dreams that she is carried on the back of a gigantic water-mammoth "that suddenly rose out of its underwater lair to start burrowing and digging through banks of black mud that flew back into her face no matter how she fought it off, protesting, and very nearly choked her." (*BBB*, p. 174) This signifies the unconscious terror of the relentless forces of self-pity and self-destructiveness. It is symbolic of her disturbed psyche. The water-mammoth represents her self-hate. She is smeared with black mud which signifies the fear of her inner process chiding her for not being able to stand up to her "shoulds." This indicates Sarah's wish to hide her identity and not to perceive her genuine self, struggling for recognition. Karen Horney describes how one patient "in his associations often used the monsters of the Beowulf legend, who emerged at night from the lake, to symbolize his self-hate." (*NHG*, p. 160) This is a move against the real self. Under its impact one loathes the idea of being oneself.

One saving grace for Sarah is that she is quite aware of the quality of her situation. She is given to self-questioning. Who was she—Mrs. Sen, married to an Indian or Mrs. Sen, the efficient secretary ? The realization that both these images are frauds, each having "a large, shadowed element of charade about it," reduces the intensity of her alienation. By asking questions one takes his first step towards action. He becomes conscious of his inner life and outward behaviour, and does not remain a passive victim of circumstances. Peter Jones introduces the terms "Actio" and "Passio" to denote these emotional states. Actio, he says is "essential not only for self-respect but ultimately for sanity."[13] Sarah feels trapped between these two selves and wishes to get out of them:

> When she briskly dealt with letters and bills in her room under the stairs, she felt an imposter but, equally, she was playing a part when she tapped her fingers to the Sitar music on Adit's records or ground spices for a curry she

> did not care to eat. She had so little command over these two charades she played each day, one in the morning at school and one in the evening at home, that she could not even tell with how much sincerity she played one role or the other. (*BBB*, p. 39)

Like Sita, Sarah too is aware of her two roles. The freedom necessary for self-identity is not fully recognised because she is only acting her roles. She is nobody when she is not dramatising her parts. She cannot even separate her two selves as they are intermingled, "if only she were allowed to keep her one role apart from the other, one play from the other, she would not feel so cut and slashed into living, bleeding pieces. Apart, apart. The enviable, cool, clear, quiet state of apartness." (*BBB*, p. 43) The discovery of the falseness of her situation is a positive step towards establishing a contact with the self. Sarah's spontaneity, which was blocked by the impasse created by these two roles she was acting out, is released. She wishes to discard the masks, and be her true and sincere self. She does not mind which identity she adopts—British or Indian—she wants it to be genuine. She wonders, "if she would ever be allowed to step off the stage, leave the theatre and enter a real world—whether English or Indian, she did not care, she wanted only its sincerity, its truth." (*BBB*, p. 39)

Will Sarah be able to adopt Indian identity when opportunity comes ? Is she ready to throw off the mask of unreality ? An opportune time comes when Adit decides to leave for India. Again, Sarah is engulfed in uncertainties. There is suspicion and doubt in her mind if Adit would help her to emerge out of her alienation; if he would be able "to lift her and to transport her to a land where she would regain warmth and personality." (*BBB*, p. 255) Here Sarah shows tendency to depend on others. She wants a prop to take her out of the rut into which her life-pattern has fallen. This is a very mild form of dependency, but Adit acquires the character of the "magic helper" discussed earlier in the case of Maya and Sita. There are moments of assurance and faith; there is also the "sharpness of fear" inside her. These contradictory feelings create considerable tension in her mind. Disintegrating forces trouble her. These thoughts, however, are not constrictive or neurotic. At long last, Sarah realises the imperative demand of her situation: she will have to forego her cultural identity in order to adopt a new culture and undergo a completely new experience. This produces a natural anxiety. The distinction between normal and neurotic anxiety is subtle: the former results from the recognition and acceptance of complexities of life. It is constructive and expanding. The latter is destructive. Natural anxiety enables a person to see the real world, to make decisions and to commit to a way of life. Sarah's anxiety helps her to grow out of her frustrating situation. Although it is painful to say good-bye to her "English self," there is a firm hope that she will "come to life" in India; it would be a "new, a different personality." (*BBB*, p. 255).

These positive thoughts have a therapeutic value for Sarah. In Sartre's *The Flies*, Oreste says to Zeus, "Human life begins on the far side of despair."[14] Sarah has undergone the experiences of depression and is ready to reach the other side which brings her a hope to find her real self. Sarah is willing to experience a new life—not only culturally or socially but psychically too. She is poised for two changes simultaneously: the birth of a child and the emergence of a novel identity.

One wonders if Sarah will be successful in recovering her self in an alien atmosphere. One also speculates if Sarah is planning another escape to get rid of certain memories which would identify her to herself. But one thinks that her self-analysis will help her in being normal. Meenakshi Mukherjee opines that she is displaced in her own country and her crisis of identity will never be solved even if she goes to India. It is true that Sarah's social or cultural identity will not be regained. But, her crisis is not irreducible. If Sarah is able to maintain the spirit of her constructive thoughts and if they are not followed by any repercussions of self-destructive feelings, she may assume responsibility for self. If she strives towards a clearer and deeper experiencing of her feelings, beliefs and wishes, outgrowing narrow, neurotic egocentricity and if she manages to relate herself to others, she will steadily gain inner certainty which comes by belonging, through active participation in life,

## III

*Voices in the City* is so much preoccupied with the nausea of Nirode and the despair of Monisha that Amla, the youngest of the Ray family, has drawn but scant attention of scholars and critics. They often limit her function in the novel to her utility in revealing the characters of others by her pungent observations. Amla is assigned a secondary place in criticism, and is seen only as a shadow of her neurotic siblings. Socially, she is caught in the whirl of Calcutta which excites her in the beginning and disgruntles her later. Psychologically, Amla is a brilliant portraiture of a rebellious young woman, eager to master life and triumph over every obstacle. Her ambitious pursuit drags her through various psychic situations till finally she establishes a contact with her real self and achieves equanimity. B. Ramachandra Rao recognizes Amla's move from revolt to conformity which he terms "surrender." One may, however, establish that Amla's conversion into a spontaneous person signifies her growth-potential. We shall ascertain, in these pages, the cause of her acquiescence and see whether Amla-Dharma relations generated it or the influence of creativity chiselled it. Monisha's suicide reveals to her the tragedy of the lost self which, according to Kierkegaard, is "sickness unto death." Amla resolves that she would not allow herself to get lost like her sister, "she knew that Monisha's death had pointed the way for her and would never allow her to lose herself." (*VC*, p. 248) This is, indeed, the starting point of her awakening. The wound accelerates the process and gives her a final view of ultimate reality. Prior to this she passes through a period of bewilderment, grappling with self-idealization and self-realization.

The disparity in Amla's idealized image and reality tosses her between two tendencies - regression and progression; and it enables us to see her internal conflicts and the external support she needs in order to grow. Basically a product of not-so-happy a home, she develops narcissistic attitude. She constantly requires reinforcement from others to counterbalance her intrinsic demands with her grandiose self. What she gets in Calcutta does not satisfy her expansive drives, and her anxieties increase. She is agitated till she gets an abundant supply of love from Dharma. The change makes her euphorically happy. She steps out of a nightmare into a dream come true. A combination of art and love, profuse approbation from Dharma and a sense of triumph help her to realise her most cherished fantasies. However, very soon the author erects emotional blocks. Relationship with Dharma becomes simply a part of the fairy-tale atmosphere. In frustration she rebels. Her anguish in this situation is the result partly of hurt pride, and partly of the discovery of her inability to control external reality. Real suffering, felt as a result of Monisha's death and self-analysis resolve her intra-psychic conflicts. In her reformation and chastened vision, the author assures us of Amla's continued growth.

Amla's basic solution is that of mastery of life. She idealizes herself as a superior being, able to fight her way through life without being morbid like Nirode or destructive like Monisha. She is conscious of the "cold, frosty love of power," (*VC*, p. 109) inherited from her mother, and she secretly embarks upon a search for glory in order to get the satisfaction of experiencing herself as her grandiose self. Indeed, Amla's first exuberance and vivacity strike a contrast to her brother and sister who have lost all faith and are marching towards self-annihilation. Amla comes to Calcutta with a vision: an anticipation to become a commercial artist. She is determined to enjoy the city, her new job and her independence. "Calcutta doesn't oppress me in the least. . . . It *excites* me," (*VC*, p. 142) she tells Aunt Lila with self-conscious buoyancy. Initially, after reading about Nirode and Monisha's corroded personalities, the third part of the novel, dealing with Amla, brings in freshness but very soon the reader detects her disillusion. When Aunt Lila utters in dismay, "you are a morbid lot, you young ones," she includes the entire generation of diseased, defiant youth, deprived of their vitality even before old age.

Critics define Amla's despair in terms of the vitiating effect of the monstrous city on a sensitive soul. Anita Desai points out that she wrote this novel to portray "the powerful impression the city created on me."[15] The pleasant and unpleasant associations are depicted in the novel denoting the beauty and the ugliness of Calcutta. Whereas the novelist agrees that she has tried to represent the duality of human activity, she is sure that there is much more in the book than mere analogy of this kind. Amla feels the impact of Calcutta. Often she regrets having come here. Staying in Bombay or going back to Kalimpong would have been a better choice. In bitter moments, she admits that it is a horrible city where one cannot be one's self. Amla has to hide her paintings to guard them as a secret. She tells Nirode:

> I have to keep things secret in this horrible city you told me was so wonderful, such a challenge. If I were back in Kalimpong, I wouldn't have minded showing them to you, I should have *liked* to show them to you. But here, here . . . here one must hide such things, cover up their weaknesses, protect their fragility, even destroy them if one doesn't want to see them get covered with filth and blood and rot. Nothing delicate can survive this. (*VC*, p. 182)

It is, nevertheless, a miscalculation to link all her troubles to the city. A liberated and intelligent woman, Amla wants, as Aunt Lila puts it, "something greater than pleasure alone, or the security of marriage alone—something more *rare*, more responsible." (*VC*, p. 145) Indeed, Amla's quest is directed towards this aspiration. She strives to master all fears and anxieties of life, so as to give meaning to it.

The self-confidence and spirit with which Amla lands in Calcutta demonstrate her capacity to enjoy life and give it a semblance of a positive approach. Aunt Lila appreciates it, "That's the spirit in which to start your career, my girl. That's what I like to see in young people—spirit." (*VC*, p. 142) This basic attitude gives Amla a resiliency and an abundance of light-heartedness. That is why, perhaps, Jit once remarks that she has a destructive quality in her. "You destroy—you destroy yourselves, and you destroy that part of others that gets so fatally involved in you. There is this—this dreadful attractiveness in your dark ways of thinking and feeling through life towards death." (*VC*, p. 175) In Nirode, it is his arrogant-vindictiveness; in Monisha, it is her remoteness. In Amla it is her own invincibility and her conviction that there is nothing she cannot win. She is secretly aware of her charm, her youth and beauty. She can impress others and she does it successfully. It is obvious from the impressions she has created on Jit, Mr. Basu and even on the obstinate and aloof Dharma. Indeed, it satisfies her pride system to be the centre of attraction, because it guarantees her uniqueness. Karen Horney discusses this attitude at some length and points out that this can be termed as "narcissism," and is one of the sub-divisions of the expansive solution. Narcissism does not simply mean an egocentric love of oneself. It stands for a broader concept when one is in love with one's idealized image. It is one of the several solutions of the conflict between expansive and self-effacing drives. A narcissist, according to Horney's theory, is gifted beyond average, he wins early distinctions and "sometimes was the favoured and admired child." (*NHG*, p. 194) Although he shows optimism, buoyancy and self-confidence beyond average, he is basically a pessimist and suffers despondency.

In Amla's personality, optimism and pessimism, joy and despair, work side by side. Even at a time when she is moving optimistically outward towards life, apparently happy and carefree, there is a "giant exhaustion growing and swelling inside her, of a feeling of sick apprehension and despair." (*VC*, p. 149) Later at a party, the "atmosphere of underlit reality, of incomplete life," (*VC*, p. 167) overwhelm her. Two contradictory emotions toss her. On one hand, she is drawn by the pleasures of Calcutta life, on the other, she is nauseated, and feels that pleasure is the "most rotten sensation in this city;" it has lost its beauty, freshness and utility. Symbolically, at the party all the people in that clustered room, appear to her as fishes, enclosed in an aquarium. This suggests, by implication, the reality of the human situation. By thematic design, Desai heightens the emotional effect. At the same party, Jit remarks that Amla and her siblings involve themselves in tragedies of their own making and reach the dead end to find some solution to life's dilemma;

> I think you all involve yourselves in the tragedies of your own making. I think you all drive yourselves deliberately into that dead end where you imagine you will find some divine solution. But there is none, not in a lifetime, all of us discover that, and we force ourselves to turn and take another road. (*VC*, p. 176)

What Jit refers to as "another road" corresponds to Erich Fromm's concept of the "other course" open to an individual who loses his human possibility. This course, discussed earlier, is devised as an escape from an unbeatable situation; it is not an answer to life. In order to overcome his loneliness and insecurity a person surrenders his individuality of the self and minimizes his anxiety. Amla feels lonely and helpless in Calcutta, but she does not seek solution by compulsive activities. She is open to awareness. Her uneasiness and despair derive from her constant but unconscious quest to protect her inner life from impoverishment. Her search is directed towards creativity.

In turning from commercial art to pure art, Amla displays her aesthetic inclination. Her profession is an amalgam of commerce and art, and defeats the very sense of creativity and beauty. In it the aesthetic and the materialistic are juxtaposed in a simultaneity which forbids communication at the deeper planes of consciousness. Amla turns to painting again and again, trying to transmute her conflicts into art. This can well be substantiated by Maslow's discussion on the creative attitude. He makes a clear distinction between abstractions and aesthetic perceptions, and observes that abstracting is an active process. It involves "selecting-rejecting." Its end-product is mathematical equation, a formula, a map or a model which is removed from the "raw reality." The end-product of an aesthetic perceiving is the full richness of reality. It gives

> the total inventory of the precept, in which everything in it is apt to be equally savoured, and in which evaluations of more important and less important tend to be given up. Here greater richness of the precept is sought for rather than greater simplifying and skeletonizing. (*FRHN*, p. 172)

Amla's profession is the routine, normal, pedestrian activity. It does not afford her the enthusiasm and the insight of the glorious moments of creativity. Nauseated by it, she turns to painting trees, insects, birds, flowers; scribbling some "nonsense rhyme" in Bengali on them. She enjoys these moments of serenity. This can be termed a brief period of "peak experience" when she loses all self-consciousness and becomes totally absorbed in non-self. The novelist describes her state lyrically:

> She was frowning in an excess of care, hesitation and mother love over this gracile, patter-footed, whisper-voiced little world that seemed to have shot down the central channel of a smooth green plantain leaf, on a stream of rainwater, to land with a splash on her window-sill, when Nirode came in. (*VC*, p. 181)

During these moments of self-forgetfulness Amla finds her authentic self, her real identity. Art becomes an exploration. Anita Desai in an interview asserts that she considers art an enquiry, a quest, a discovery, not an escape. Amla plumbs the underlying psychic conflicts by moving away from the relentless pressure of the world around her. It is her refusal to be depersonalized by the dehumanizing effects of contemporary life. Her struggle is to connect her self with nature in order to feel whole. It is, indeed, interesting to note that while nature lends her equilibrium, it uncovers for Dharma a new meaning in perennial man, through her.

Relationship with Dharma is instrumental in giving a renewed vision to Amla. After her first meeting with Dharma, Amla reorients herself. Modelling for him makes her "translucent with joy and overflowing with a sense of love and reward." (*VC*, p. 210) Her real self, eclipsed so far by her grandiose self, tries to emerge. Anita Desai presents it symbolically as the worm crawling out of Amla's ring in dreams. Dharma paints the ring in Amla's finger with the worm creeping out "of her nightmare to push its insidious head out of the painted stone and arouse, in the painted Amla, that very turbulence of disgust, revulsion and fear that so often assailed the dreaming

Amla." (*VC*, p. 213) This indicates fear of the real self. Dharma's love and art influence her. She correlates the self and the world and overcomes her anxiety. The novelist describes Amla's experiences as the peak of her season of love, as a perfection in which "lay all the joy and the sense of being the right person in the right place that love should have made diffuse and scattered gently through the season." (*VC*, p. 217)

Amla-Dharma relationship, however, is not well-defined for either. It is just a balance between reality and hallucination, creating a precarious situation in which Dharma cannot give her the tangibility or permanence. Amla is aware of this deficiency. Her dreams represent her inner conflict. The white birds she dreams of stand for reality. For the dreaming Amla, reality is fascinating but it chides her. She, the love-lorn maiden, symbolised by the arching palms, is unable to meet her sparkling reflection in the water. This denotes, by implication, the impossibility of being and living her grandiose self. It indicates that she has to find her real self, however horrified she may be of it. All this works at the unconscious level.

Theirs is, in fact, not love but only "psychic symbiotic union;"[16] a pattern of relationship in which two persons come closer, their bodies remain independent, but psychologically they develop attachment. There are "active" and "passive" forms of symbiotic fusions. In Dharma's case it is active; he enjoys his sway over Amla and feels inflated and enhanced by her idolatory. He thus escapes his aloneness. In the case of Amla, it is passive; she derives pleasure by being an integral part of Dharma's art; he fulfills her need for admiration; in him she finds a responsive appreciating audience. She endows him with mysterious faculties, he becomes the "magic helper" to prop her and guide her through life. These are the projections and externalization of her own imagined qualities.

The question is: why does Amla, so young, independent, and spirited fall a prey to her passions, particularly for a man in Dharma's position? It is because, being a "narcissistic" subtype of the expansive drives, Amla's idealized self needs to be a centre of attention and attraction. Dharma fulfills it. Flabbergasted by her unbearable isolation in Calcutta, she drifts towards Dharma, makes him an integral part of her life, renounces her integrity and depends on a force outside herself. This idolatory is significant for Dharma also. He achieves a graceful interaction between humility and the pride of creativeness. As an artist he is able to see the human possibilities and limitations. His portraits get depth and he feels gratified to see the archetypal man. Her transparent inner self gives him fresh insight. He admits that she made him see "what the subconscious does to an impressionable creature, how much more power it has on them than sun and circumstances put together. And this is the revelation that made me . . . begin on a new era." (*VC*, p. 223)

Amla's breaking away from Dharma appears as enigmatic as her attachment for him. Critics believe that she feels hurt to learn of Dharma's callousness towards his only daughter and that she leaves him in disgust. A close study of Amla's character reveals that the reasons for her decision to leave Dharma are not so simplistic. Amla is mainly distressed by her own conflicts—her pride and irritability. Pride: because she is so significant in his life as to awaken his dormant talents. Irritability; because he is lost in his art and is distracted from her. These conflicts so far controlled, explode in the face of reality. Her reactions are both strong and instant.

First, we try to understand Dharma's so-called cruelty to his daughter. When she wriggles out of his protective "chrysalis" he reacts with a feeling of helplessness and impotence. He tells Amla that he did not want his daughter to grow, "I wanted her the same, always the same, beside me." (*VC*, p. 227) When she struggled out of his hold to marry a cousin, he turns callous, disowns her and in an attempt to save himself from the assault of self-hate withdraws to his secluded suburb, away from the city. This feeds his ego. It is a manifestation of power over the girl, and reminds us of Maya's father who sacrifices his daughter "at the altar of his own image."[17] Same type of unsavoury sensations trouble Dharma now, as Amla chooses to walk out of his life. This time he turns from his seclusion to the full hubbub of life in Calcutta. His old friends, admirers, critics, buyers of his art-pieces, agents all serve to gratify his intrinsic need for triumph. As Nirode observes, "new self-centredness was eclipsing Dharma's once brilliantly clear and detached vision." (*VC*, p. 224) Unfortunately, Dharma bargains for something mediocre when art opened the doors for self-realization. His compulsive need for power and expansion remain unchanged, and he pursues them to reaffirm his superiority.

Coming back to Amla again, she finds him as an erring mortal and the image she has of him as someone mysterious and forbidding, is shattered. If he could reject his daughter, he could well enough shut her out from his life. His distractions towards his creative work are a sufficient indication that she has outlived her utility for him. Amla dreads the truth because as Maslow points out truth carries with it responsibilities and that it is an anxiety-producing state. The easiest course is to evade the consciousness of truth. In Amla's case, truth dawns on her with impunity: that she is treading dangerous grounds, that Dharma is, after all, committed to his wife and society, that he is a conformist, not possessing the strength to enrich her life by giving her the joy of love. Aunt Lila was probably right in her remark that Dharma was "using" something in Amla. This hurts her pride.

In an attempt to plunge into the dull routine of life which she had tried to beautify with love and art, she leaves him. She tears up the invitation to Dharma's exhibition and goes with Jit for horse-race. This is her regression choice. It is movement backward and suggests symbolically her sickening view of life as a gamble. Here, she sees the stark reality—death. She also visualises the actuality of life—life is a race, one has to participate in it and strive to win. One who fumbles and falls remains an "outsider," invaded by the forces of self-hate, alienation and self-destruction. In the shadow of death she discovers the value of life. She opts for progression. This is a significant move towards self-actualization. Amla is tossed between the pressures of her neurotic drives and her affirmative will-power. Her journey to and fro indicates her self-doubts. As Nirode observes in the novel, journey entails an expense of energy both of mind and body. Human potential lies in making the journey worth the expense. One only hopes that with Monisha's death, Amla grapples with her authentic self and maintains the poise she displays at the end of the novel. Between Nirode's neurotic outbursts and mother's withdrawal, Amla stands as an emerging self.

## NOTES

1. Atma Ram, "A view of *Where Shall We Go This Summer?*" *Journal of Indian Writing in English*, pp. 74-80.
2. Atma Ram, "Interview with Anita Desai," pp. 21-33.
3. S.S. Anant, "Conflict Resolution through Belongingness," *Manas*, 26, Nos. 1-2 (1979), pp. 63-64.
4. Fromm, *Escape from Freedom*, pp. 140-41.
5. S.M. Jourard, *The Transparent Self: Self Disclosure and Well-Being* (New Jersey: D. Van Nostrand, 1964), p. 101.
6. May Sarton, *Journal of a Solitude* (New York: W.W. Norton, 1963), p. 60.
7. S. Krishnamurthy Aithal and Rashmi Aithal, "East-West Encounter in Four Indo-English Novels," *ACLALS Bulletin*, Sixth Series, No. 1 (Nov. 1982), pp. 1-16.
8. Meenakshi Mukherjee, "The Theme of Displacement in Anita Desai and Kamala Markandaya," *World Literature Written in English*, 17, No. 1 (April 1978), pp. 225-33.
9. Alvin Toffler, *Future Shock* (London: The Bodley Head, 1970), p. 13.
10. J.H. Van den Berge, "The Changing Nature of Man," Introduction to *A Historical Psychology* (New York: W.W. Norton, 1961).
11. Kamala Markandaya, *Some Inner Fury* (London; Putman, 1955), p. 285.

12. Paul Tillich, *The Courage to Be* (New Haven: Yale University Press, 1952), Chapter 6.
13. Peter Jones, *Philosophy and the Novel* (Oxford: Clarendon, 1975), p. 85.
14. Jean-Paul Sartre, *No Exit and Three Other Plays* (New York: Knopf, 1949), p. 123.
15. Srivastava, "Interview."
16. *The Art of Loving*, p. 23.
17. Jasbir Jain, *Stairs to the Attic*, p. 117.

# 6

# THE SERAPHIC VISION

The melodrama enacted all through by Desai-personages from Maya to Sita, including Nirode, finds its hangover in Bim in *Clear Light of Day*, though in a milder form. It trickles down to Deven, the protagonist of *In Custody*. Bim suffers under her drives, appears as irrationally angry as Sita at times, as sentimental as Maya, and yet she grows out of these sickly sentiments in time to locate herself in a chaotic world of over-sensitivity. In her, there is a synthesis of emotions and knowledge, a fusion of facts and fiction: qualities that enable her gain a relative freedom from her private hell.

## I

Bim, the chief protagonist of *Clear Light of Day*, is an interesting study of the self in transition. She possesses many attributes that Third Force psychologists associate with healthy human development. Although she is often unsteady, oscillating between alienation and confirmation, almost losing her self in the struggle, in the end she discovers the structure of her own consciousness and achieves wholeness. The melancholia that shatters her balance for the twenty long years is a measure of her sense of failure of life to honour her aspirations. But, nonetheless, her courage and intellectual strength remain unaffected.

Many readers refer to this positive streak in Bim's character. Meenakshi Mukherjee, for example, credits her with a change of heart, calmness and love. Another critic finds her a "failed quester" who desired to conquer the world but who ends up by conquering herself. Bim develops the "awareness of time and its importance in human life," and strives "to be whole, to be sane amidst all decay, destruction and death."[1] R. S. Sharma alludes to Bim's "transcendence." He recognizes her efforts to evaluate her own self by rejecting all that had hindered her growth into a truly liberated soul. Thus, she goes towards the realization of a new self. It is, however, arguable that, though Bim is a victim of circumstances, she is basically a self-actualizing person in Maslovian terms. Self-alienating forces work on her psyche for long, assuming almost pathological proportions. In her weak moments she resorts to resignation, wishing to run away from life, but these forces do not completely overwhelm her. Our inner nature, though weak, never disappears: "Even though denied, it persists underground forever pressing for actualization." (*TPB*, p. 4). Despite her frustrations, failures and pains, Bim's vision increasingly embodies a transfiguration of her sense of alienation into a new consciousness of wholeness through psychic renewal.

The first glimpse we get of Bim is that of a pathetic heroine, an aging spinster, rotting in the decadent old house in Old Delhi, the city that does not change, that only decays, "a great cemetery, every house a tomb." (*CLD*, p. 5) Her sister's yearly visit brings her little comfort, only scorching memory of a past she would fein forget. The author affirms that the family reunion is "only partly successful" as "there are many sour notes among the happy ones."[2] What makes Bim so hysterically ascerbic is the situation she is placed in, not only by an unrelenting fate but by her brother Raja also. Raja absolves himself of his family responsibilities and, on top of it, has the audacity to write a self-righteous letter.

We meet a Bim, irate and unforgiving, sarcastic and bitterly distraught. She tends to free herself from her past, to impose a cynical restriction on all her wishes and to close all chapters of childhood and youth as periods of "dullness, boredom and waiting." (*CLD*, p. 4) This is a typical neurotic solution to turn away from people, and it reveals her main concern to prevent any further disappointment in life. She erroneously discovers that safety and peace can be obtained by leading a life of stoicism. This lack of passion, want of emotions and excitement, is also known as apathy. H. S. Sullivan observes that this is a strange situation: "It is a way used to survive defeat without material damage, although if it endures too long one is damaged by the passage of time. Apathy seems to me to be a miracle of protection by which a personality in utter fiasco rests until it can do something else."[3] When this strategy does not work, Bim slips into a vindictive-aggressive rage. These intra-psychic conflicts produce alienation. Nevertheless, Bim does not lose the basic charm and strength of her personality: she is maternally affectionate towards her students; she is still admired by Bakul, silently, for her "decision, firmness and resolve"; (*CLD*, p. 18) loved by Dr. Biswas for her courage and fortitude; and is adored by her readers for the unique ability to laugh off her pains. Slowly out of the vignette of a disgruntled spinster, emerges a woman of seraphic vision of the clear light of day, of clear sunshine.

The vision of life enfolds in itself various qualities attributable to a mentally healthy person. A growth-oriented individual has clear and efficient perceptions. It happens because "the effect of wish, desire, prejudice upon perception . . . should be very much less in healthy people than in sick." (*MP*, p. 154) Bim has the unique quality of vivid perception. The Lodhi Garden episode of the bees is meaningful in this context. Bim does not grudge Tara for having abandoned her to the attack. Instead, her reaction is "you couldn't help it." The chivalry is natural to an adolescent girl wanting to become a "heroine." It may be an act of natural sisterly love. Besides, it requires clarity of cognizance to accept a situation ungrudgingly.

It would be fruitful to look at the formative influences that make or mar Bim's psyche. Raja, Bim, Tara and Baba, have a home, a family, if presence of parents and roof overhead is the notion. For, the parents are too engrossed in their Roshanara Club and cards. There is hardly any exchange between the children and the parents. They could certainly go haywire like the Ray-children in *Voices in the City*, for want of parental affection, but for the benign presence of Mira-*Masi*, a mother surrogate. Raja and Bim do not appear to be in need of a mother, too busy as they are in their robust outdoor activities. But, the presence is there, and they could turn to her whenever need be. Not for nothing does Bim often think of her as "the tree, she was the soil, she was the earth." (*CLD*, p. 111) She is saviour for Tara who clings to her for protection against the elder too, Raja and Bim. Much of the emotional crisis is warded off, just because Mira-*Masi*, a *good* mother is there. Baba, the retarded child, gets emotional security; Tara, the weakling of the three changes over from the protective embrace of Mira-*Masi* to that of Bakul, and is happy with her life. The detrimental home affects Raja. He turns an escapist, a self-centred, dreamy romantic, shrugs off all responsibilities, like the parents and settles down to an ordinary life—the crass, the banal of mundane reality. It is Bim who, with a vast treasure of read-literature stacked in her brain—Eliot, Byron, Swinburne, romantic books, adventure stories, history—shifts between past memories and present realities, shuttle-cocks between her self-alienating forces and her strength of spirit and mind. How she emerges out of these, is the question.

Bim's awareness and mental alertness are revealed in her decision not to enter into a marriage with a person like Dr. Biswas. A lucrative offer, particularly for a young girl in Bim's situation, it could be a romantic experience. She could have responded positively to the Doctor's courting. At first, she is swayed, yet she at once realises that he is not a man made for her. She is flabbergasted at Biswas's remark:

> Now I understand why you do not wish to marry. You have dedicated your life to others—to your sick brother and your aged aunt and, your little brother who will be dependent on you all his life. You have sacrificed your own life for them. (*CLD*, p. 97)

Angry at being so grossly misjudged. Bim reacts vehemently. She presses her hands together as if to break something. But soon she drowns "rage and frustration . . . with laughter at such grotesque misunderstanding, and her tangled emotions twisted her face and shook her, shook the thought of Biswas out of her." (*CLD*, p. 97) Her neurotic struggle to close all doors on the past and run away from conflict commences with this breaking up of self-image.

A spirited and talented student, Bim is a companion of Raja in his robust boyish activities. She finds herself in the image of a great heroine. In their childhood game of questions, her inevitable reply to what she would be when she grows up, is always that she will become a heroine. Her real-life heroic figures are Joan of Arc and Florence Nightingale. She chides Tara when the latter avoids going to hospitals on charity Thursdays, "otherwise what good will you ever be ? If you can't even do this little bit for the poor, what will you ever be able to do when you grow up ?" (*CLD*, p. 126) Bim admires her heroines and wants to emulate them. "I won't marry. . . . I shall work, I shall *do* things," (*CLD*, p. 140) she tells Tara. Her resolution is two-fronged: it shows her aggressive spirit to let down Tara who has no ambition at all; it also displays her sincere urge to be independent, to *do* something. The sincerity of her determination has the seed of self-actualizing tendencies; but her aggressiveness changes, imperceptibly, into a glorified image.

Bim's glorified self-image is that of heroic figure who can achieve something in life. The striving to be really great like others indicates growth, but, trouble arises when instead of the real self the idealized self-image is upheld. In this case, it is important to have a glimpse of their home atmosphere. With the mounting dissatisfaction in her family, the growing adolescents—Tara and Bim—"become infected with some of Raja's restlessness." (*CLD*, p. 130) Bim grows ambitious and Tara finds an escape in Bakul's love. Her desire to "be a mother and knit for her babies" is realised. Bakul's training and love save her from mental wreckage. Mira-*Masi's* words, said unwittingly though, seem to have prophetic proportions. "There, there, you'll see you grow up to be exactly what you want to be, and I very much doubt if Bim and Raja will be what they say they will be." (*CLD*, p. 112) Raja achieves his goal by second hand means. Having married Hyder Ali's daughter, the Byronic romantic feels complacent that he has emulated his boyhood hero, Hyder Ali Sahib. Bim, stuck with her abnormal brother, Baba, is entangled. She feels lost, and also inferior to Raja and Tara who have achieved what they wanted. Bim is not jealous, the futility of her desires tortures her.

Bim's main tendency is to grab power and glory. Whenever she fails to attain it, she turns to vindictive triumph. Her victim is Tara. By humiliating her or inflicting pain on her, she derives a sense of achievement. Bim's childhood ideal has been Raja. Quite unconscious of the sex differences, Bim becomes as mischievous as a boy. When Raja grows up and withdraws, she does not comprehend the change that "his maleness and his years were forcing him to withdraw from the cacoon-cosiness spun by his aunt and his sisters out of their femaleness and lack—or surfeit—of years, she grew resentful." (*CLD*, p. 118) The novelist describes in detail how Bim is led to "be cruel to Tara." She clips Tara's long hair because the latter longed for curls. This one cynical act speaks volumes for Bim's "unconscious impulse to defeat others in personal relations." (*NHG*, p. 27) One could let go it as childhood mischief if such acts were not repeated then and even later. Middle-aged Bim's occasional remarks are cynical enough to inflict deep pain on Tara. She is cruel and sarcastic at times, and Tara recognises "the moment when Bim went too far with which all their encounters had ended throughout their childhood. . . ." (*CLD*, p. 7) Indeed, Bim is always thinking in terms of triumph.

Triumph for young Bim means to be at par with Raja. To wear his clothes, to puff his cigarette secretly, to fly kites with him are some of her passions in the field of physical activities. In the intellectual arena, their paths diverge as they grow up. Boys's books like *Robin Hood* and *Beau Geste* that set Raja's imagination on fire, have no fascination for Bim. Nor can she enjoy the light romances dragging her "into the underworld of semi-consciousness" like Tara. Bim cultivates a higher taste in her reading. Gibbon's *Decline and Fall* inspires Raja's admiration and awe at the intellectual depth of his sister. But, apparently he ridicules her for her lack of imagination. Bim feels hurt and puzzled. This, naturally, creates "a gap between them, a trough or a channel that the books they shared did not bridge." (*CLD*, p. 121)

Sociologically, to emulate and equal masculinity is a tragedy of a woman's life. Ferdinand Lundberg and Marginia Farnham, for instance, consider all feminine striving for achievement as mere envy. For them, such an upbringing is a distortion of character which is "driving women steadily deeper into personal conflicts soluble only by psychotherapy."[4] Helen Deutsch in her study of women's psychology almost agrees with these and states that intellectuality is a betrayal of a woman's basic feminine nature. An intellectual woman, she observes, is "masculinised; in her, warm intuitive knowledge has yielded to cold unproductive thinking."[5] We may apply this view to Indian social set-up as well. The Hindu social code sees external ambition in women as detrimental and unnatural. Anita Desai also affirms in an interview with Jasbir Jain that in Indian society of the early nineteen forties, of which she is writing in this novel, "certainly one was aware that men had a different kind of life open to them which was entirely shut to girls. Girls at that time didn't even visualise having any kind of independent will to choose for themselves." Sociological factors regard Bim's high ideals of service only as a "sacrifice for the family." Judged by this conventional social matrix her sublime ambition is reduced to a pathetic search. Her spirited volition to "*do* something" collides with the social set-up, igniting conflicts. Inner frictions intensify Bim's need for supremacy. Soon it acquires a compulsive character. Bim realises that the world does not recognize her as Florence Nightingale or Joan of Arc; and that life is full of reality. To counter this reality, she makes claims on life. Bim, who takes Tara's marriage so gracefully and happily, reacts violently when Raja leaves. Her reaction is understandable: Raja, the eldest must bear the family burden. But, she tends to exaggerate Raja's actions. Her words contain much bitterness; Raja is "selfish," "he is too rich to be interesting anymore, too fat, too successful. Rich, fat and successful people are *boring*. I'm not interested, Tara." *(CLD*, p. 143) Her sullenness intimidates Tara. Bim succeeds in projecting an exaggerated view of her suffering. She thus, asserts her claims on life. Somewhere deep down this intense frustation lies the undercurrent of fear—fear of being left alone.

The outward reaction of fear is anger. Bim stores it long enough to damage her psychic condition. She is angry with Raja for his letter. But the pent up rancour and rage simmer within her for long without finding a way out. She develops psychosomatic symptoms like talking loudly to herself and gesturing with hands. One afternoon, the volcano bursts. Her "anger swelled and spread, acquiring demonic proportions." (*CLD*, p. 163) Baba is made the target, "to vent her hurt, and pain and frustration on." Once the rage was spent, Bim's purview is cleared. It has a therapeutic value. With the purgation of emotions, all doors are opened by self-examination.

With her rejuvenated perception, Bim comprehends the reality of Raja's character as well as the myth of his heroic image. Since childhood, she has seen her adored brother as a young Byron—a hero and poet—writing stormy poems, fighting for a cause. Lord Byron's stories help in the formation of this image. This is an "ideal construct." Raja *must* be heroic. Raja *must* live upto his image. This is how Bim concludes. But when he bargains for something lesser, she feels cheated. Without realising Raja's real character and his intrinsic capabilities Bim breeds, for twenty long years, the rancour for her broken ideal. She derides Raja, she surmises that he must be unhappy. To a surprised Tara she tells that Raja was not meant for the inferior things of life—family, money, business. That is not

> what Raja had wanted from life. He doesn't need a hobby, he needs a vocation. He knows he has given his up. Just given up what used to be his vocation, turned it into a silly, laughable little hobby. . . .(*CLD*, p. 145)

In fact, all her bitterness towards him is the outcome of her own erroneous picture.

When Bim sees Raja in a clear light, actually he has always been, she unravels a mystery about herself. She reads Raja's poems again. His juvenile verses reveal mediocrity. He was never an original poet, but a mere imitating, repetitive scribbler mouthing Swinburne and Byron and Iqbal. It was an adolescent romanticism. In his poems she could no longer find the heroic, Byronic Raja she so much adored:

> . . . not the Raja now and not the young Raja, the child Raja. For the poems were really derivative. On each of them she could clearly see the influence of the poets he loved and copied. There was no image, no metaphor, no turn of phrase that was original. Each was a meticulous imitation of what he had read, memorised and recited. He had made no effort to break the iron rings of cliches, he had seemed content to link them, ring to ring. . . . He had not, it seemed, really set out to startle by originality, to burst open the literary world as a new star, fresh and vivid. One could see in them only a wish to emulate and to step where his heroes had stepped before him. (*CLD*, p. 168)

Bim discerns that Raja's ambitions have been "modest and unassertive." This demise of the hero has another aspect, too. If Raja is not a hero, Bim is not a heroine either. The false self-image she has had guarded so well, dissolves in the process. The emergence of the new self provides a dependable barometer to re-evaluate and re-assess herself.

In speaking about wholeness, humanist psychologists encourage man to become more aware of the possibility of his growth as a person. Man is an end, rather than a means. The goal, the Greek Oracles set for him, "Know Thyself" and what the Hindu philosophy also substantiates as "*Atmanam Vidhi*" is a great pointer towards recognising his true self, above fragmentations. Bim's personality achieves a continuity in time as she develops an ability to integrate the past and the future. This does not mean that Bim forgets her past. Past cannot be given up, memory cannot be wiped out. Individual personality is made up of memories, habits and reactions. Past is to be "digested," so that it assimilates with the personality and does not remain alien to it. Past exists *now* in the person, future as "*now* exists in the person in the form of ideals, hopes, duties, tasks, plans, goals, unrealized potentials, mission, fate, destiny. . . ." (*TPB*, p. 214) Bim assimilates her past and future with her present and gets ready for peak experience.

The self-actualizing peak experience does not come to Bim so easily or smoothly. For twenty years she suffers under alienating forces. There is a long period of self-glorification, the urge to be on the "top," to "rule others" as Jaya remarks. During this period her intrinsic qualities—intelligence, spirit of adventure, and natural vitality—have been eclipsed by her actualised self-image. We see her often speaking of herself with a succinct pride, "I could have been a nurse—or a matron—in a plague hospital. I can handle it all," (*CLD*, p. 85) she tells Dr. Biswas. Behind this statement, there lies a compulsive need to elicit confirmation of her devotion. She prides in her roles of a nurse, a supporter, the head of the family. As long as she is praised by people, she enjoys it all, feeling satisfied. But, slowly and gradually, everybody takes her sacrifices for granted; even Raja leaves. She passes into a state of despondency and self-pity.

The first inkling of self-pity we get in her passing thought "there is never anybody except me," when Raja tells her to go and find out the welfare of the Hyder Alis. Later, it takes a deeper colouring. At the peak point of desperation she accuses her father:

> For all father cared, I could have grown up illiterate and—and cooked for my living or swept. So I had to teach myself history, and teach myself to teach. But father never realised—and Raja dosen't realise. . . . (*CLD*, p. 155)

Probably she forgets that their father did not care for any of his children. Likewise, the resolution to remain unmarried and be self-sufficient has been her independent act.

As long as Bim is high on the wave of success, she does not understand well the situation she is placed in. When she cannot master life any longer she looks for peace of mind by blocking consciousness and shrinking all sensitivity to nothingness. Bim's untidiness symbolically represents her lack of zest for life. The bright adolescent girl, who worked deliberately and consciously to stand first in the examination and win laurels, is now turned into a middle-aged spinster, wearing faded maxi, living in a dilapidated old house, with an unkempt garden. Everything about her reflects the decadence of mind. It is like Nanda Kaul's dictum that when a woman lives alone, her house should mirror her state of mind. The lines from *The Pillow Book of Sei Shongon* suit her well enough. Her sister, Tara, is shocked at the condition of the "dead old house," as if dishevelled by a storm. Bim regales in it and asserts that it indicates the passage of time, time that is gone and will not come back.

She is afraid of her past as she cannot relate it to her present. She wants to forget it because it means involvement. All she wishes is to lead a will-less existence. Under this facade of quiet martyrdom, is a "subdued rebel." Bim turns her rebellion against her inner self. Outwardly, she spends all her fury on Baba and Tara, but inwardly she is enraged at her own weakness in having to ask for help from Bakul or Raja. She remarks: "How my students would laugh at me . . . if they knew how badly handicapped I still am, how I myself haven't been able to manage on my own—they'd laugh, wouldn't they? They'd despise me." (*CLD*, p. 155) In reality, her students would not despise her, she is afraid that she will loathe herself for her weakness. This is her dread of vacuousness. She becomes angry with herself, and her rebellion becomes an inward process. It is "an evolution than a revolution," which helps in liberating a person from his neurotic compulsions.

Bim's psychic movement from self-alientation to self-realization is the journey of a self temporarily befogged by compulsive drives. Some critics feel that the transformation of Bim from sickness to health is unconvincing. Growth is a continuous process, and the real self of man is not completely lost. It is always present and struggles to come up at the slightest opportunity. Bim's character, all through the novel, shows some positive qualities Circumstances and her inability to see what she really wants from life impede her growth and diffuse her energies. Slowly as the narrative unfolds, we see her changed vision. She attains internal freedom; she is liberated from her twisted vision and her confused values. By unifying the diverse fragments of her world into a unified whole she achieves wholeness. In Henry James's *The Portrait of a Lady* the concern shown by Henrietta over Isabel's possibility of drifting from the realities of life to the ivory tower of luxuries and amid self-centred high-ups, is significant to understand the universal human constant. "The peril," says Henrietta to Isabel Archer, "for you is that you live too much in the world of your own dreams. You're not enough in contact with reality—with the toiling, striving, suffering, I even say sinning, world that surrounds you."[6] Likewise, till Bim establishes a viable contact with her surroundings and her brothers and sister, she is in peril. As soon as she achieves this, she is liberated.

When Bim feels one with her siblings, she grasps the depth of love binding her to them:

> There could be no love deep and full and wide than this one, she knows. No other love had started so far back in time and had had so much time in which to grow and spread. They were really all parts of her, inseparable, so many aspects of her as she was of them, so that the anger and disappointment she felt in them was only the anger and disappointment she felt at herself. Whatever hurt they felt, she felt. Whatever diminished them, diminished her. What attacked them attacked her. Nor was there anyone else on earth whom she was willing to forgive, more readily or completely, or defend more instinctively and instantly. She could hardly believe, at that moment that she would live on after they did or they would continue after she had ended. If such an unimaginable phenomenon could take place, then surely they could remain flawed, damaged for life. The wholeness of the pattern, its perfection, would be gone. (*CLD*, p. 165)

This new vision implies the acceptance of the inner core of her being. This self-searching or "turning inward in a meditative way" is a significant quality of a growth-oriented person as he, thus, solves many of his problems.

One of the most important things about Maslow's self-actualizing person is his spontaneity: "Pure spontaneity consists of free, uninhibited, uncontrolled, trusting, unpremeditated expression of the self." We find that self-knowledge and self-acceptance lead Bim to trust herself. Emerson considers faith in oneself as a mark of genius:

> To believe your own thought, to believe that what is true for you in your private heart is true for all men—that is genius. Speak your talent, conviction, and it shall be the universal sense; for always the inmost becomes the outmost. . . . A man should learn to detect and watch that gleam of light which flashes across his mind from within, more than the lustre of the firmament of bards and sages.[7]

Bim discovers the "gleam of light" when she sees the wholeness of the pattern in the moments of her intense consciousness. The unrestricted act of understanding means the discovery of the relationship between herself and her brothers and sisters.

The metaphor of awakening works all through. It broadens the interpretation of the novel. It is an important romantic metaphor for the emergence of the self into a new life, an image that appears in the works of transcendentalists like Emerson, Whitman and Thoreau. *Clear Light of Day* opens with the Koel calling, symbolic of the day and waking up. The motifs of sleep, afternoon nap and waking up run through the narrative till finally Bim, after the harrowing day spent in rage and the night spent in tearing herself free from the burden of the past, awakens to greet her nieces. Awakening posits a double world—the one within and the one without. It prepares Bim for her final aesthetic experience.

Bim's moments of inner delight come on the musical evening arranged by the Misras. Soothing tunes of music flowing from the Guru of Mulk, bring out a harmony between the subject and the object, the perceiver and the perceived. Through this harmony, complete identification of the inner and the outer world is established. As Fredrich Schiller points out, it is only through beauty that man makes his way to freedom. The aged singer's sharp but sad voice brought out the "storms and rages and pains of his life." (*CLD*, p. 182) The pain, frustrations and beauty of that voice consists in it the revelation of the timeless within the conditions imposed by time. In the experience of artistic beauty, the abstract and the sensuous lead to a greater recognition. Iqbal, Eliot, the Guru, his music and Raja, all become one in her absorption. Bim sees through the limitations of human perception, beyond time. She enjoys the comfort and the solace of this experience. The aesthetic contemplation leads Bim from inconclusive temporal experience to the comprehension of the eternal unity. The abstract becomes concrete and vibrates with ennobling feeling:

> With her inner eye she saw how her own house and its particular history linked and contained her as well as her whole family with all their separate histories and experiences —not binding them within some dead and artless cell but giving them the soil in which to send down their roots, and food to make them grow and spread, reach out to new experiences and new lives, but always drawing from the same soil, the same seed of darkness. That soil contained all time, past and future in it. It was dark with time, rich with time. It was where her deepest self lived, and the deepest selves of her sister and brothers and all those who shared that time with her. (*CLD*, p. 182)

Bim's experience supports the Hegelian view that the realm of Fine Arts is the realm of absolute spirit.

Bim rises above the limitations of the ego-centric self. She unconditions her mind by becoming totally attentive to a holistic experience. The perception becomes relatively self-forgetful and ego-transcending. During such self-validating moments, her quest for identity end; she finds the "real me" (to use a phrase of William James). The crisis of her adolescence and the problems of her adulthood that had staggered her, are now substituted by a coherent self.

This experience, does not make Bim paragon of rarefied visions. She is a character in the process of fulfilling her self, rising above the limitations of pettiness. Maslow believes that a very important theoretical conclusion arising out of his study of self-actualizing people is that the dichotomies usually seen as part of human nature, i.e. masculine-feminine, head-heart, maturity-immaturity, are resolved and are merged with each other to give unity to a self-actualizing individual. Dichotomies express the condition of a mind still locked in bitterness. In Bim's case, all dualities vanish, separation between the observer and the observed comes to an end and conflicts end. Bim connects the artistic observation of life with its reality. It is her progression towards the uniqueness of personality to which Deven is a robust heir.

II

Deven, the protagonist of *In Custody* (1984) presents the stage next to Bim's in psychic balance and wholeness. A clear awareness of the betrayals he has inevitably fallen into and an honest recognition of human limitations, help him to break away from the contemporary wasteland and move towards understanding and totality. The positive vision, bequeathed to him by Bim, displays his choice of existence over annihilation. On a number of counts, both physical and psychological, Deven's insight provides a motif for a way out of the psychic impasse through self-affirmation. Deven substitutes judgment from within for opinions from without, self-awareness, for the hostile tensions of his situation, and the resultant inner conflicts. One understands the unsolved confusion and worry, that render him helpless and thwart his expectations. However, spontaneous self-realization dilutes the effect of the self-alienating forces. Life becomes a palpable experience in which one has to engage in a process of give and take. This approach to life reduces the tension of an outrageous situation. The novel acquires the dimensions of an intransient work of art. Anita Desai dramatises Deven's moments of crisis by reflecting the banality of the surrounding life.

The novel unfolds the story of credulous and disingenuous Deven Sharma, who is swayed by an idea of creating a work of his lifetime, but is, unfortunately, defeated by his own helplessness. A temporary lecturer in Hindi in a private college in Mirpore, a suburb of Delhi, Deven is interested in Urdu Literature. As the novel opens, we see his friend Murad, now editor of an Urdu magazine, requesting Deven to interview

Nur Shahjehanbadi, for a special number of his forthcoming issue. "Deven's hand fluttered on to his knees as he melted at the suggestion and felt a glow creep through him at the thought of writing something in the language which had been his first language. . . . The glow was also caused by pride . . . at being asked to contribute a piece by the editor of what he took to be a leading Urdu journal." (*IC*, p. 16) The rest of the narrative shifts between Deven's success and failure, his enthusiasm and hesitancy, and the final disaster he lands into. Various forces work to deter and to help him alternately till finally he stands at a cross-road, not knowing where to turn to. In the end he finds strength in his inner self and resolves to face life as it comes to him.

The prime characteristics of Deven that attract our attention are his helplessness, humility, suffering and nobility. Socio-economic factors colour his personality and mould his psyche. The son of a debilitated, asthmatic school-teacher, Deven belongs to a lower middle-class family. As a child, he has watched closely the bitter disappointments of his mother and the "apologetic smile" of his father for his failure in measuring up to her expectations. Obviously, these familial and social factors generate into him powerful compliant tendencies. We have its glimpse in his encounter with Murad in Deven's college. While Muard is free and frank even in an alien atmosphere where he is only a casual visitor, Deven, who belongs to it, appears subdued and inferior by contrast. He becomes conscious and nervous while talking to Murad: "He tried to wriggle out of Murad's grasp unobtrusively so as not to offend him." (*IC*, p. 9) He feels embarrassed and cannot tolerate his students staring at him. The forces working in him side by side show his tendency to subordinate himself to the wishes of others. A conflicting situation arises when he has to meet the demands of his "shoulds"—on the one hand, he should guard his image of a sober teacher, on the other, he should measure up to his friendship. He cannot annoy Murad because it would jeopardise his need for love and affection. But he feels guilty when his students watch him with Murad, in an exuberant mood. His idealized image of himself is that of an upright teacher in the college, a humble man in society outside and a victimized self in his home, turning aggressive often.

On the familial front, Deven finds himself as an angry self. The repressive atmosphere of a lower-middle-class ethos offer him no suitable avenues of recognition. He is a gifted young man whose imagination has been fired by the glories of the Urdu poetry. The harsh realities of life produce in him intense feelings of frustration and resentment and force him to adopt different solutions to cope with his difficulties. Deven is aware of his personal incompetency, that, he is incapable of fulfilling his wife's desires and dreams on the material level. Like his father he feels apologetic because he cannot do better. This helplessness prevails in his attitude towards his life in general and towards his family in particular. He lives with a sense of defeat and failure:

> He understood because, like her, he had been defeated too; like her, he was a victim. Although each understood the secret truth about the other, it did not bring about any closeness of spirit, any comradeship, because they also sensed that two victims; ought to avoid each other, not yoke together their joint disappointments. A victim does not look to help from another victim; he looks for a redeemer. At least Deven had his poetry; she had nothing, and so there was an added accusation and bitterness in her look. (*IC*, p. 68)

Deven feels inferior and contemptible not only due to Sarla's attitude but also owing to his diffused sense of failure. Overtly, his irritability and anger with Sarla appear to be the outcome of his hurt male ego. Deep down, his rage is, in a way, an externalization of self-hate, born out of an unconscious self-accusation. He reproaches himself for his inadequacy to make his distinction in life: "... all he could measure up to was this—this shabby house, its dirty corners, its wretchedness and lovelessness." (*IC*, p. 67) What he had secretly dreamt of was "the world of drama and revolving lights and feasts and furies," (*IC*, p. 67) something like Nur's world. The impossibility of translating his dream into reality frustrates him. In society, with friends, he cannot revolt. It is basically alien to his compliant nature. At home he imposes his superiority, turning aggressive, and intimidating Sarla. His rebellion consists of getting furious with her, flinging dishes, tearing shirts and expressing his rage in countless minor actions. He protests against Sarla's disappointment, "he was out to wreck it, take his revenge upon her for harbouring it. Why should it blight his existence that had once shown promise and had a future ?" (*IC*, pp. 68-69) In revolting against Sarla's dreams, he in fact, tries to ward off the onslaught of his self-contempt.

The externalization of his self-accusations helps Deven in relieving his inner tension to some extent. Outside his home, he adopts self-minimizing as a protective measure. He tries to extricate sympathy from Murad by being apologetic and humble. This is well explicated by the cowering manner and tone of Deven's pleadings, " . . . you have seen how hard it is to survive in this position. If I knew a way to change my situation, I would do it but—what is there to do?" (*IC*, p. 14) It could be argued that this scene is just a *tete-a-tete* between two friends and has nothing self-degrading in it. But, obviously the flow of their conversation reveals Deven's repeated attempts to gain Murad's sympathy. The author also comments that in the desperation of his circumstances he tried to elicit compassion, and said something which he would not have. "All through his childhood and youth he had known only one way to deal with life and that was to lie low and remain invisible." (*IC*, p. 14)

Reducing himself to a zero, Deven engages himself in the shrinking process. Self-minimizing is debilitating. A person gripped by it cannot make assertive or expansive moves. Deven avoids triumph or success because it is "presumptuous." He places taboos on his thoughts and feelings. So acute and unconscious is his self-minimizing that he dubs himself a fool in his first encounter with Nur. To Nur's irritated query "Fool, are you a fool," Deven's ready response is "Sir, I am ! I am !" (*IC*, p. 38). This cannot be termed only as his confused state of mind nor can it be assigned to his oblivious joy at finding himself in Nur's presence. It is an indication of his moronic condition due to the effect of shrinking his personality to a nullity. The situation is comic and imparts a lighter touch to the novel's rhetoric. At a deeper level it is an unconscious awe at having to face greatness personified. The immediate (unconscious) reaction is to cut short his presumptuousness and feel small and ineffective. This suits his temperament—a suffering, victimized self as he is. After his first visit to Nur, Deven decides to abandon the idea of having to continue the interview. This decision has reasons: first, the sordid aspect of Nur's personal life is too unpalatable for him. Second, forsaking the project is a face-saving device which suits his temperament. It simplifies his existence, "reduced it once again to a pure emptiness with which he knew how to cope, having coped so long. He had made a timely escape from complexities with which he would not have known how to contend. Compared to the horror of that threat, this grey anonymity was sweet." (*IC*, p. 71)

The ambivalence in Deven's thoughts and actions deserve attention. On the one hand, he decides not to involve himself any further with this affair; on the other, he is driven to Nur with the compulsions of a sleep-walker. This can be justified on several counts. That he loves Nur and has a devotional attitude towards him is beyond dispute. But, whereas his conscious mind is repulsed by Nur, the man, his unconscious still propels him to Nur, the poet. In the face of all odds, despite humiliations, Deven reaches the poet in all devotion, sitting cross-legged at his feet, caressing his slippers. In fact, Nur, the poet, represents to Deven all that he has idealized in himself. He does not wish to tarnish this image because if it is damaged, Deven will be doomed. It will mean demise of Deven's glorified self. He comes to Nur again and again to resurrect his hero from the debris of his previous meeting. Deven's image of Nur is hallowed by a dignity and glory which in actuality the poet lacks. "He had pictured him living either surrounded by elderly, sage and dignified litterateurs or else entirely alone, in divine isolation." (*IC*, p. 51) Contrary to this, he meets a senile and debilitated old man presiding over a court of louts and lechers.

Deven's visit to Nur is his quest, an attempt to identify the intangible world of spirit to the tangible, visible world. He is not aware that a search for the ideal to the exclusion of the visible is in itself self-defeating. Thomas Wolfe observes that the deepest search of man's life is the quest for father. It is not the father of his flesh but "the image of strength and wisdom external to his need and superior to his hunger, to which the belief and power of his own life could be united."[8] Deven does not know that in his quest for greatness, the ordinary and the dismal, the crass and the sordid aspects of life cannot be evaded. They constitute reality. Only towards the end, trapped from all sides, does he recognize his true self when he rises above his confusion and finds a joyous affirmation in life. Till this moment Deven feels entrapped because he tries to bridge the gap between his real self and his idealized self, by turning to Nur.

Deven's dependence on Nur weakens his inner personality. He is not aware that all his powers to feel, think or act are related to an outside factor. Deven is unable to express his individual potential. He cannot stand alone. His whole life is tinged with helpless drives to comprehend himself through Nur who is greatness personified. Fromm goes on to describe the disappointments of a man whose magic helper falls short of his expectations. Since this expectation is an illusory one, any actual person is inevitably disappointing. The result is that he breeds a resentment for his own enslavement to this ideal magic helper, and encounters the resultant conflicts within himself. This leads to a blockage of spontaneity. Lacking spontaneous responses, Deven entraps himself further into automatic and compulsive activities.

This is characterized by Deven's tendency to surrender his individuality. His self-effacing drives force him to follow Murad. It is a condition of a constant crossfire. If Deven accedes to Murad's requests, he feels weak and angry with himself; if he does not, he is gripped by his own worthlessness because it entails having betrayed a friend. "He is damned if he does something, and he is damned if he does not." (*NHG*, p. 221) Murad is cunning. He has caught Deven's weak points and knows how to manipulate things to his own advantage. To a casual reader Deven appears a simpleton not being able to see through Murad's tricks, but he is not. Deven has little faith in his friend. He is aware that Murad can deceive him, and that he is capable of sacrificing Deven's interest for a selfish gain.

At one place in the novel he broods that it has been foolish on his part to trust Murad, "considering the full range of his mood and shifts in temper, his contradictions and discrepancies, he wondered why he had trusted his word, taken it seriously enough. . . ." (*IC*, p. 34)

It is an irony that as soon as Deven decides to free himself from Nur and Murad, he is much dragged in. Either Murad's contrived letters sent through Nur, or his coaxing, works on Deven's mind. He reaches out to Nur to strengthen his intrinsic needs for appreciation and love. During their first encounter he tries to impress Nur, so as to get nearer him. The first line that comes to Deven's mind is "Through suffering I shall atone for my sins !" This is significant. As a self-effacing man, he tends to glorify his suffering, because "suffering *per se* appears as the proof of nobility." (*NHG*, p. 236) Deven's efforts are directed to prove his worth so that Nur accepts him in his circle. While reciting Nur's verses he feels as if he were his own mother and Nur, a child:

> He understood completely, in these minutes, how it must feel to be a mother, a woman. He had not known before such intimacy, such intense closeness as existed in that dark and shaded room. . . . He was also aware, with the welling up of a drop of sadness that now rose and trickled through him, moistly, that this moment that contained such perfection of feeling, unblemished and immaculate, could not last, must break and disperse. (*IC*, p. 45)

Feeling like mother denotes tenderness. It is a height of lovable qualities Deven cultivates in himself. He idealizes himself and wishes to perpetuate these minutes of perfection. He cannot speculate that these meetings will land him into difficulties.

Deven has an ambition—to get his mongraph published and to reach somewhere in the literary field, but he has not a pushing personality. He often has nightmares in which he sees himself struggling to reach some destination but "was repeatedly waylaid and deflected. . . . His feet seemed to be enmeshed in the sticky net of the nightmare that would not let him escape at any level of consciousness." (*IC*, p. 31) The dream symbolizes his repressed expansive trends and dormant ambitions forcing him forward but his self-minimizing drives ensnaring him. Same conflicts mark his everyday behaviour. His every move is hampered by his self-abnegating undercurrents. His impatience at this dichotomy is expressed through train symbolism. The whistle of the train irritates him because it reminds him of the conflict within him. The train calling over vast spaces beckons him to move on: "It promised nothing, it merely reminded prisoners of their bars, mocked them in their cells." (*IC*, p. 132) In *Voices in the City*, Nirode is also disturbed by the whistles of trains and the hooters of ships. As discussed in Chapter IV, his inability to start the journey indicates the uncertainties of his temperament. Like Nirode, Deven also lacks will-power to act, to get moving and reach a destination. The difference lies in the fact that while Nirode's case is desperate, Deven still retains the capacity to wish which is symbolic of the progressive element in man. As William Lynch points out, "to wish is the most human act."[9] Deven's difficulty arises because he lacks self-confidence; he needs a prop to goad him and to support him.

Luckily for Deven, help comes readily from Murad, Siddiqui, Nur's first wife and his own students. What he does not realise is that each is out to take advanatage of him. He is an easy prey to their tactics. He needs them and looks up to them helplessly for encouragement and support, and feels relieved when his burden is shared. Self-pity weakens him further. "No one ever listens to me"; "My hard work leads nowhere, to nothing. Nothing," (*IC*, p. 185) are a few of his expressions typifying his defeatism. A sense of discomfiture hangs about him persistently. He is assailed by doubts and his reply is "I can't," to every new venture. When Murad chides him for such trepidations, he gains a semblance of confidence and struggles to make some headway in the project. His timidity and inefficacy go to such an extent that Deven cannot even buy a tape-recorder, leave alone operating it. He lets himself be deceived in the deal. It suits him to have someone to depend upon: Murad is there for bargaining, Chiku comes handy to operate the machine. This is mental lethargy. It shows that Deven has lost his capacity to defend his self-interests. While he undertakes the task, the dichotomy in his basic nature persists. The ambitious part of his temperament demands that the interview should be perfect but, the self-defeating side makes him nervous, so much so that he thinks in terms of abandoning it. It is a dilemma, a vacillation between "the devil and the deep sea, between having to reach the peak and having to keep himself down." (*NHG*, p. 318) Murad's words in case of Deven are revealing when he reproaches Deven for letting himself be carried away by the work. Synthesis is essential between the ideal and the real, between human potentialities and possibilities, between compulsions and spontaneity. Unfortunately, the balance tilts; Deven focuses his vision on the glorious end-product and is inveigled. Fortunately, he maintains the capacity to hear the inner signals, and saves himself from cognitive losses and diminutions of humanness.

The original strength of the real self which, though lost temporarily, can be found and refurbished (or reinforced) to spontaneous growth. This is wrought not by any sudden or magic change in the psyche but by self-realization. The diminutive process is reversible and if one, at any stage, recovers the ability to cognize the inner signals, one can regain the real self. For Deven, this moment comes with the realization that he has to find his own strength and not depend on others. "Oddly enough, the certainty that he could expect no more help from Murad had a calming effect upon him. Perhaps when everyone had cut him off and he was absolutely alone, he would begin to find himself and his own strength." (*IC*, pp. 189-90) Throughout the narrative, Deven feels like a trapped animal. Marriage, family and even his friendship with Nur appear to him a cage. This is the time when his vision is not cleared. He is ensnared by his own illusions of the pseudo-self. Once he discovers the ineluctable reality of existence, that positive freedom can be gained by removing the blockage on inner dynamism of life, he is able to live as an independent individual. Thought at the highest level is illuminating and when a person understands his inner being he becomes light to himself, an integrated human being, not looking to somebody else to tell you what to do, what to think and how to think. When all support is withdrawn, Deven explores his own potentialities that he can stand all by himself. His strength lies within, not without. This discovery is a *sine qua non* of inner directives guiding him to take cue from within.

Deven's self-discovery at the final moment of crises is not abrupt, nor is it impossible, although it appears to be sudden. The foregoing discussion reveals his highly compliant basic nature. The author also portrays him timid and lacking in dynamism. But, Deven is not one of those self-alienated individuals who lose the capacity to feel, strive and cope with life; who yearn to express themselves but find their voices dry. There is no doubt that Deven has his share of intense conflicts. He suffers what Maslow terms "Jonah Complex", meaning thereby a tendency to run away from one's best talents or mission in life. One can get out of this situation with the help of self-awareness and self-analysis. Deven emerges out of his Jonah complex during his epiphanic moments. He regains his ability to take decision and shoulder his responsibility. Taking decision and accepting responsibility are the distinctive forms of consciousness in those individuals who are moving towards self-realization, integration and maturity. Once Deven recognizes his responsibility, after Murad's perfidy, he is filled with an "iron of resistance and he felt steady, straight." (*IC*, p. 190)

For a brief moment after this, Deven undergoes a semblance of "Peak experience." Sitting on the empty bench, he loses his self-consciousness, forgets his surroundings, his pain of having been betrayed. Everything around him becomes "clearer and sharper . . . cool, high-minded and remote." (*IC*, p. 192) He comprehends the secret of the trans-temporal nature of art and literature. Artistic works are not the chronicles of social reality, but they transcend it to project the realm of future possibilities. An aesthetic experience enables a perceiver to reach beyond the conditions of his existence. Art is an instrument of liberation but it cannot be expected to offer solutions to every problem, as mathematics or the sciences do. "If art, if poetry, could be made to submit their answers, not merely to contain them within perfect, unblemished shapes but to release them and make them available," (*IC*, p. 192) it will burst and lose its real character. Deven's quest ends in value-discovery. For a short span he tosses between diminutive drives and growth potentiality, but ultimately the duality vanishes in his epiphany and he sees reality in a broader perspective. Facts of life and the premium placed on value, fuse together in his thoughts and this helps him come out of his depression. This is the process of acceptance. From being afraid of ourselves we move towards resignation and then towards thinking. Understanding of our failings enables us to see full humanness as a glory.

Deven does not attain this pre-vision of glory all of a sudden. There is an oscillation, at times he goes back to his mood of anxiety and despondence. He wishes to make amends for his humiliating behaviour with his wife but feels too proud to let loose his hold on her. He once again approaches Siddiqui and cowers before him. Till finally, perfections of art and imperfections of human nature, reality and illusion, all stand clearly illuminated in the morning glory after a sleepless night. After this aesthetic experience his self-consciousness is transformed into spontaneity. He subscribes to the Hegelian view that the realm of fine arts is the domain of absolute spirit. He separates the two personalities of Nur—the poet and the man. An artist is the child of his age, under the corrupting influence of his time, but his art remains untainted. Deven rejuvenates his vision with the cognizance that his friendship with Nur is not a trap but a liberation. He has received the gift of Nur's poetry and "that meant he was custodian of Nur's very soul and spirit. It was a great distinction. He could not deny or abandon that under any pressure." (*IC*, p. 204) This aesthetic experience has a great cathartic influence on him: he reorients himself in the objective world and establishes a self-world relationship. Psycho-therapists believe that if one is able to relate himself to the world directly, experientially, with his senses alive, he can overcome his isolation and anxiety. Identified, thus, with the historicity of life, he builds a communion of consciousness with Nur and reaches out for an experience of human solidarity and inter-dependence. His friendship with Nur turns into a pure unimaginable relationship overcoming its craven and crass characteristic:

> That friendship still existed, even if there had been a muddle, a misunderstanding. He had imagined he was

> taking Nur's poetry into safe custody, and not realized that if he was to be custodian of Nur's genius, then Nur would become his custodian and place him in custody too. This alliance could be considered an unendurable burden—or else a shining honour. Both demanded an equal strength. (*IC*, p. 203)

Deven's transformation is effected through the medium of an aesthetic experience and is reminiscent of Mr. Bose's vision of early morning pigeon flight in Anita Desai's short story "Pigeons at Daybreak." Mr. Bose forgets his dull and drab existence and the pain of his illness at the divine sight. Likewise, Harish in the short story "Surface Textures," spends ecstatic moments at the rocky area near the river which he finds perfect in its exquisite roughness of shape and design. Deven's temporal experiences are exchanged for the calm of eternal form. He reaches a wholeness of self; achieves the spontaneity when he marches away from a self-created trap to the joyous affirmation of life which is a pre-condition of positive freedom.

In the character of Deven, Anita Desai studies at once a timid and ineffectual but growth-oriented person who shows self-confidence, clarity of vision and equilibrium. She manages to balance the self-alienating forces with actualizing qualities and offers a convincing portrait. The hero displays some healthy attributes. Though throughout the novel he is a weak and pale personality and is tossed by self-effacing drives, all his feebleness is submerged at the crucial moment of self-scrutiny. His awakening typifies coherence and completeness.

Deven has not achieved any *metahuman* qualities nor has he transcended ordinary humanness. He has simply risen above the ordinary differences and has gained the attitude of recognition of the essential solidarity and mutuality of human beings. His vision is not altogether a superfluous appendage nor is his self-actualization contrived, because it is inherent in the aesthetic and thematic pattern of the novel. As the novel's rhetoric suggests, the new Deven at the end is not an illusion but a reality. This is also represented symbolically when, while rushing homewards, Deven stops only to pull a thorn from his foot. It is a significant act implying his decision to march towards a higher goal beset with thorns. Deven has predominant self-effacing drives but the author's deft handling of his value system identifies him with growth-oriented individuals. He is, at no stage, severed completely from his intentionality at the wish level. It takes him long, but he finds his set of values and his aims in life. He acquires transparency when there is self-acceptance and a confidence that his real self will be accepted and that he has the courage and strength to handle rejection. Finally, Deven transcends his personal problems and gains an awareness of the existential problem of man. He accepts the human condition as it is and reaches an existential dimension of personality.

## NOTES

1. Shantha Krishnaswamy, *The Woman in Indian Fiction in English (1950-80)*, p. 279.
2. Ramesh K. Srivastava, "Anita Desai at Work: An Interview," p. 225.
3. Harry Stack Sullivan, *The Psychiatric Interview* (New York: W.W. Norton, 1954), p. 184.
4. Ferdinand Lundberg and Marginia Farnham, *Modern Woman: The Lost Sex* (1947; rpt. New York: Gosset Dunlop, 1978), pp. 235-36.
5. Helen Deutsch, *The Psychology of Women: A Psychological Interpretation* (1944; rpt. New York: Bantam, 1973), I, pp. 280-81.
6. Henry James, *The Portrait of a Lady* (London: Everyman's Library, 1983), p. 202.
7. Emerson, "Self-Reliance," p. 59.
8. Thomas Wolfe, *The Story of a Novel*, quoted in *Thomas Wolfe* by Elizabeth Nowell (New York: Doubleday, 1960), p. 27
9. William F. Lynch, from an unpublished paper delivered at a conference in New York, 1964. Quoted by Rollo May, in *Love and Will*, p. 212.

# 7

# FROM DARKNESS TO LIGHT

Anita Desai is a great analyst of the human mind, a creator of brilliant characters, and an astute interpreter of life. She presents a gallery of vivid and realistic portraits. The motivational system of her personages works in the peculiar manner suited to their environment and their basic needs. When we grasp her character's psychology, we begin to see them as *human* with their weaknesses and potentialities. They are, indeed, caught in the web of their own compulsions, but cannot be regarded as "haunted protagonists"[1] who do not come to grips with life. When understood psychologically, we begin to visualise their ambitions, disappointments and loneliness as real. They react to their troubles with tragic intensity. By her fictional rendering of neurotic behaviour, interaction and solution, the novelist not only plumbs human nature but also helps us to grasp their inner reality intuitively. What psychologists and social scientists treat objectively, by abstract analysis, Anita Desai provides subjectively by her aesthetic portrayal.

Many readers appreciate Anita Desai's achievement in creating characters independent of social or political issues, but they concentrate mainly on the thematic aspects of her works. The psychological intricacies of the behaviour of her protagonists, their struggle to find a meaning in life symbolise the concern of modern man with the eternal human situation which speaks of the changed perspective of writers in depicting characters. Anita Desai's art is not traditional: her personages are engaged in contemplation, not action. Notwithstanding this limitation, she has been successful in capturing and holding the attention of her readers by her narrative skill. Her freshness and spontaneity indicate her rich creative faculty. She creates a character in order to tell a tale and embody her vision of life.

In studying the works of literature in the light of Horneyan and Maslovian taxonomy, we do not detach characters from their aesthetic and thematic patterns. A novel "is not simply mimesis; it is a story told from a certain moral and intellectual point of view and from a certain emotional distance."[3] Anita Desai's characters are not case studies of neurosis, nor are they evolutionary histories of psychological phenomenon. They are living individuals, interested in life with its hopes, dejections, and chaotic flow. They are moved by the aesthetics of existence, "whatever is beautiful and good, whatever has glory and power, is only a portion of the divine radiance." (*The Gita*, X, 41) Nevertheless, the trouble with some of them is that they, at times, take a wrong path and perpetuate their neurosis.

From this point of view, a majority of her characters—Maya, Monisha, Nirode, Raka, Nanda—live either in illusions by retreating into fabrication and fantasy, or show their reluctance to face reality: they live in self-imposed solitary confinement. Then, there are characters who compromise with life—Sita, Sarah, Amla, Bim and Deven. Although they have their conflicts, they manage to transcend their personal problems. Amla suffers existential crisis but soon decides that she will not allow herself to be lost like her sister. This affirmation is spontaneous. Bim accepts her present, and linking it with her past, marches ahead towards a bright future. In Sita and Bim, there is, at least, a resolution to affirm life. Deven incorporates a more dynamic and integrated approach. After a sleepless night, he is able to segregate lived reality from art. The salvation for him lies in the aesthetics of life. His everyday life is sufficiently alive to liberate his drive for self-realization. The growing urge for self-discovery in Desai's characters thus exhibits the growth potential of her protagonists as also the ever-developing vision of their creator.

In order to reveal the beauty and ugliness of life, Anita Desai deploys characters having acute sensitivity to its grandeur as well as sordidness. She is not a visionary or a mystic, but an artist who shows, in Hardy's words, the "sorriness underlying the grandest things and the grandeur underlying the sorriest things."[3] Their anguish and dilemmas impinge upon their selves. Since she analyses the inner workings of the mind of her characters, she does not overload her works with details of physical traits of personalities. Her primary occupation in all her works, is not how one gets along with others, but with oneself. The basic problem, she says, is "how to exist in society, and yet maintain one's individuality. . . ." She presents action through the minds of these people shifting their mental time backward and forward. Virginia Woolf calls it her tunnelling process by which she tells the past by instalments. This is the stream-of-consciousness method of delineating a character. This mode of characterization "achieves by depth what traditional method achieves by extension." It

> provides a method of presenting character outside time and place; in the double sense that, first, it separates the presentation of consciousness from the chronological sequence of events, and second, it enables the quality of a given state of mind to be investigated so completely, by means of pursuing to their end the remote mental association and suggestions, that we do not need to wait for time to make the potential actual before we can see the whole.[4]

A scrutiny of Anita Desai's art shows that the novelist is growth-oriented. The development from her first heroine, Maya, to her latest creation, Deven, is the story of a steady ascent towards self-realization. One discovers this expanding vision of authenticity in her short stories where her characters show an ability to integrate their disintegrated personalities in moments of epiphany. Her artist-protagonists, or those with an artistic inclination, manage to see beauty and harmony through the sordidness of life. In Anita Desai the urge for self-expression is in itself a powerful drive towards self-actualization. As Horney points out, "the creative urge itself and the creative power can stem only from his (artist's) desire for self-realization and the energies in its service." (*NHG*, p. 332)

Perhaps her own urge for self-realization, bequeathed to some of her protagonists in the shape of their artistic visions, is responsible for the fullness of compassion in her fiction. There is a rich vitality in an ordinary life, even. Some of her characters are free of spirits, who, dissatisfied with routine of ordinary world, break away from their existing life-patterns, only to realise that family and social ties cannot be substituted. The apparently stoic Nirode, recluse-by-choice Nanda Kaul, seeking some kind of fulfilment in their lonely existence, are drawn to their environment again and again. For some of Desai's characters the realisation comes sooner or later that individual freedom must create some kind of a new relationship. After all, apathy, inertia and uninventiveness are not the answers to life. This fact is obvious in George Eliot too, where the movement toward individual freedom is reversed to find a relationship with society. If Desai's Maya, Monisha, Nirode are the denizens of a social void, her Amla, Sarah, Bim and Deven move towards a reconnection with other people.

Keeping in view the seriousness of their self-alienation and the possibility of self-actualization, Anita Desai's characters may be studied in four groups. In the first category we place Maya and Monisha, who are sensitive and are pitted against insensitive spouses. Their defence strategies are, however, not alike. Maya is a case of severe psychosis; she is a morbidly dependent person who values love and sex beyond everything else in the world. When Gautama does not stand up to her expectations, she turns violent. Her self-hate comes to the surface turning self-destructive. She first kills him and then commits suicide. Monisha, on the contrary, is a withdrawn creature. She weaves a glorified picture of herself as a superior being, much above her in-laws. When charged with theft, her self-image suffers a shattering blow, her neurotic pride is hurt, and self-contempt overpowers her. Under its impact she sets fire to herself. The two solutions adopted by Maya and Monisha—morbid dependency and resignation—are the outcome of detrimental home conditions. Through these moves the protagonists try to defend themselves from their pathogenic environment. We feel that their alienation and consequent trouble are not due to marital disharmony, but their marital discord emanates from their own inner conflicts.

Then, there are cases of neurosis: Nirode, Nanda and Raka. None of the three commits suicide, though each is on the brink of it. Nirode's troubles start with his conflicting demands and their defensive solutions. He is intrinsically aggressive-vindictive. When he cannot hold on to his idealized image, he turns to resignation. Monisha's death hurts his neurotic pride; further, his mother's rejection works havoc on his psyche. The fear of losing her affection disturbs him. The image of Mother *Kali*, the destructive as well as creative forces, converge in his mind and he sees his mother as *Kali*. This is an archetypal image since mother *Kali* remains in the collective unconscious of Indians as a race. Nanda's death-wish owes to the failure of her self-effacing solution. She hankers after love. All her life she makes sacrifices to get attention and love, and is ready to engage once again in a period of dedication when Raka comes. She is torn by conflicts when her detachment clashes with her self-effacement. Nanda dies as her real self struggles to overpower her glorified self. The knowledge that her life has been one of lies and make-believes shatters her self-image. Our contention is that Nirode is not a case of Oedipus complex and Nanda is not an aloof person: they are both victims of their self-alienation.

The destructive effect of self-alienation is much less discernible in Sita and Sarah. In the beginning Sita has compulsive drives as she is almost a neurotic. However, later she compromises with life. For her the answer to life's problems does not lie in running away from it, but in facing it bravely. The revelation helps her to integrate herself. Sarah faces social and psychological alienation, though she looks forward to a fruitful period in India. These are not fully self-actualizing individuals. Their brief moments of self-discovery and affirmation give us a hope that they can gain more spontaneity of feelings in later life provided they do not shift from one neurotic solution to the other. We find greater clarity of perception in Bim, Amla and Deven. Bim's rage in the early part of the novel is almost neurotic but her vision soon acquires authenticity. She finds her lost self and achieves self-realization. Amla also has an affirming faith in life. Deven is trapped in his self-created mess. Socially, he is in a precarious position and suffers humiliation but, indications of an acceptance of life on mental level, are there.

Her characters may not be fully healthy, self-actualized individuals, but all of them are not outright sickly, insane or morbid. Some of them have vitality and aliveness. In the process of individuation they reveal self-strength and a tendency to emerge out of their isolation, insecurity and anxiety, and gain a kind of closeness and solidarity.

Swami Vivekananda, in one of his moments of self-analysis, categorized two types of people: the sensitive and the strong-nerved. Whereas the former are always given to fight and take a stand, the latter accept life as it is; the former are unhappy, the latter are often happy:

> There are two sorts of persons in world—the one strong-nerved, quiet, yielding to nature, not given to much imagination, yet good, kind, sweet, etc. . . . There are others, again, with high-strung nerves, tremendously imaginative, with intense feelings—always going high and coming down the next moment. For them there is no happiness. The first class will have almost an even tenor of happiness. The second will have run between ecstacy and misery.[5]

This statement comes nearer Desai's ideas about her characters who "clear the decks for battle" and accept to fight. In her Sarah, Sita, Amla, even the compromise with life implies a reconciliation after recognizing the self. There is a harmony between their reason and experience. Bim and Deven too cannot dodge their problems completely. They undergo conflicts and after much agony recover themselves. The presentation of struggle of the "sensitive" ones, running between agony and ecstasy, is Desai's forte.

In the process, she enables us to see those recesses of the human psyche which generally elude interpretation and comprehension. Hers is a "serio-problematic representation" of life. Socially, her field is limited to the class she comprehends adequately. Except for Deven and Nirode, her protagonists are women for she understands their mental, moral and social struggles. Within this field, she manages to lend complexities to her people and portray them in the "context of the human struggle." They possess traits of personality which probably they themselves do not comprehend. The conspicuous outward change in their behaviour is the outcome of an unobservable inward process.

Out of the mundane day-to-day happenings, Anita Desai creates a world in which the inner and the outer selves aspire for a harmony. Where this state is realised, the ending marks a happy synthesis of reason and unreason, reality and unreality. The reward is: achievement of wholeness. The deeper dimensions, of which the characters themselves are not wholly aware, come to the forefront. The totality of a human experience imparts a metaphysical perspective to her fiction. Her writings are largely reflective, and mirror, by implication, the social conditions affecting the male and female (as well as child) characters in traditional as also in modern Indian society.

It would be unfair to read these novels as melodramas and the characters as bundles of neurosis. They are individuals in their own right. They have their own artistic inclinations, their reading cultures. What they read and what tickles their consciousness even after they have stopped reading, is significant to know them. There are Gautama and Monisha, both influenced by the *Gita*. Both interpret the chapter on detachment: each according to his requirement. Commensurate with her sensuous bent of mind, Maya is moved to the core by Urdu verses. Apart from the *Gita*, Monisha's wardrobe is stacked with Dostoevsky, Kafka and Hopkins. Sita is tickled, again and again by D.H. Lawrence's verse. Probably, his "pristine consciousness" akin to Maslow's "real self" is an indication of his characters's search for fulfilment, because it is a fact that his fiction has "offered a new source of energy and inspiration to humanists." Bim's reading is vast and covers a wide range from boys's adventure books to Gibbon's volumes on history. Here, fact and fiction, reason and unreason merge into her. A lover of history and a teacher of history, Bim is able to muse on the lot of humans, and carve a path for herself. Lines from Eliot's *Four Quartets* signify "time," the fourth dimension. The obsession of Nanda Kaul for emptiness is matched by the book she loves, *The Pillow Book of Sei Shonagon*. Sita's urge to go to Manori is like Margaret Atwood's *Surfacing*, wherein the protagonist leaves the city in search of her father. Both Sita and Atwood's heroine are questers. Although these novels deal with psychological transformation, the resemblance ends here.

The aesthetic value of Anita Desai's works is projected through a pattern and rhythm, lending harmony to her writing. The novelist attaches importance to "pattern and rhythm." Her patterns are based on her assertion that the "human condition" does not change. Her profound feelings spring from her art of creating human beings caught in the terror of facing existence with all its sickening reality. Lost in the labyrinth of their personal psychological problems, her characters are seen labouring to come to grips with life. Their troubles are not superficial, but ingrained in them since childhood. As children most of them are allowed to stay in an atmosphere of magic and superstition. A denizen of the world of myth, magic and fantasy, the child projects his own feelings into an objective external world. Everyday realities disappear and take the colour of the child's affective state. If this "primary process" of perception persists in adult life, the individual continues to show an "infantile" mode of behaviour. Maya's father, a fatalist lets her daughter live in a world of superstitions. Likewise, Sita is surrounded by magic. Maya fails to assimilate the inner and outer realities, because she deals with the everyday reality by her primary process. Nanda and Raka too are inclined towards the fantastic. The supremacy of primary processes lead these characters to the distorted view of outside reality, create in them an impaired ability to grasp the real meaning of external relationship.

Through an artistic way of projecting life as it is—chequered emotionally as well as spiritually—Anita Desai shows the ability of her narrative art to maintain contact with life. Her treatment of modern themes like alienation, isolation, quest for wholeness, is authentic. She reworks the psychological material in a variety of contexts. The conflict in her characters, their defence mechanism and their psychic life are objectified in the novels in a disguised form. The psychic configuration expressed through her characters, their memories, dreams, hopes and fears interwoven with the themes and structural patterns provide multiple dimensions to her work. Her sensitivity is shaped by her creative vision which is not limited to the surface comprehension of the everyday reality. The artistic apprehension of life marks the essential aesthetics of her art. If it is "the immense richness of material which life provides," she draws from this source, frames these experiences in a pattern and puts it in the timeless completeness of art. The fictional central consciousness works in association with the rich sensitivity and sensations of her own individual vision and thus unifies action. It is the art—painting—that helps Dharma and Amla to restore their faith in life. It is life itself, seen in the light of art—poetry—which intensifies Sita's wish to explore and confront the inner and outer worlds. Likewise, Bim reconciles the emotional, social and familial wholeness by experiencing a living personal relationship. Anita Desai's vision displays a kind of formal unity as her later works reach dènouement. Her central characters are continually engaged in a quest. There is a final affirmation of life's resilience. She employs the psychological time to achieve an ideal of artistic wholeness.

Anita Desai's men and women are not heroes or heroines, absolute in their strength or devoid of human weaknesses. They are ordinary beings with normal human limitations. Indeed, Desai's world is not an "artistic utopia." The great illuminative power of her fiction lies in its mimetic presentation of experience. These rebel-victims are not the outcome of an eccentric vision of the author but they are indicative of the emergence of this disquieting stance which modern literature stands to project. Highly distinctive in their motivations, manners and methods, her personages constitute a significant contribution to the Indian novel in English.

## NOTES

1. Harish Raizada, "The Haunted Protagonists of Anita Desai," *Perspectives on Anita Desai*, ed. Ramesh K. Srivastava, pp. 17-30.
2. Bernard J. Paris, *A Psychological Approach to Fiction*, p. 282.
3. Thomas Hardy, "Notebook Entry." Quoted by Miriam Allott in *Novelists on the Novel*, p. 132.
4. David Daiches, *The Novel and the Modern World* (Chicago: Chicago University Press, 1960), p. 24.
5. Letter to Mary Hale, in *The Yogas and Other Works*, ed. Nikhilananda (New York: Ramakrishna-Vivekananda Centre, 1953), p. 165.

# BIBLIOGRAPHY

## I. PRIMARY SOURCES

### Anita Desai's Works

(i) Novels

*Cry, the Peacock.* London: Peter Owen, 1963. Calcutta: Rupa Publishers, 1964. Delhi: Orient Paperbacks, 1980.

*Tipatul Panulai.* Rumania: Colectia Meridiane, 1966 (in Rumanian).

*Voices in the City.* London: Peter Owen, 1965. Delhi: Hind Pocket Books, 1968.

*Bye-Bye, Blackbird.* Delhi: Hind Pocket Books, 1971.

*Where Shall We Go This Summer ?* Delhi: Vikas Publishing House, 1975. Delhi: Orient Paperbacks, 1982.

*Fire on the Mountain.* London: William Heinemann, 1978. New York: Harper and Row, 1977. Delhi: Allied, 1977. Sweden: Trivi, 1980. Harmondsworth: King Penguin, 1983.

*Clear Light of Day.* London: William Heinemann, 1980. New York: Harper and Row, 1980. Harmondsworth: King Penguin, 1983.

*In Custody,* London: William Heinemann, 1984.

(ii) For Children

*The Peacock Garden*. Bombay: India Book House, 1974. London: William Heinemann, 1979.

*Cat on a Houseboat*. Bombay: Orient Longman, 1976.

*Village by the Sea*. London: William Heinemann, 1982. Delhi: Allied, 1983.

(iii) Short Stories

*Games at Twilight*. London: William Heinemann, 1978. Bombay: Allied, 1978. New York: Harper and Row, 1980. Sweden: Trivi, 1980. Harmondsworth: Penguin, 1982. The anthology includes "Pineapple Cake," "Games at Twilight," "Private Tuition by Mr. Bose," "Studies in the Park," "Surface Texture," "Sale," "The Accompanist," "A Devoted Son," "The Farewell Party," "Pigeons at Day-break," "Scholar and Gypsy."

(iv) Uncollected Short Stories

"Circus Cat, Alley Cat." Delhi: *Thought*, 1957. Collected in M.C. Gabriel and Gwen Gabriel, eds., *A Selection of Modern Indian Short Stories*. Delhi: Sidhartha, 1968, pp. 95-98.

"How Gentle is the Mist." *The Illustrated Weekly of India*, 1958.

"Tea with the Maharani." *Envoy*, 4 (January-February 1959).

"Grand Mother." *Writers Workshop Miscellany*, 1 (August 1960).

"An Examination." *Writers Workshop Miscellany*, 3 (1960).

"Ghost House." *Quest* (Jan.-March, 1961).

"Mr. Bose's Private Bliss." *Envoy*, 6 (May-June 1961).

"Private Tuition by Mr. Bose." Delhi: *Indian Literature*, 1970.

"To Sell a Picture." *Writers Workshop Miscellany*, 6 (1961).

"Descent from the Roof-top." *The Illustrated Weekly of India*, 91, 4 Jan. 1970, pp. 36-39.

"Surface Texture." *Femina*, 1974.

"The Accompanist." *Quest*, 1975.

(v) Essays, Articles, Reviews

"Calcutta Kaleidoscope." *The Illustrated Weekly of India*, 1958.

"Gangtok." London: *Envoy*, 1959.

"A Kulu Christmas." London: *Envoy*, 1959.

"Pilgrimage." *The Illustrated Weekly of India*, 1966.

"Women Writers." *Quest*, No. 65, April-June 1970, pp. 39-43.

"The Indian Writers' Problems." *The Literary Criterion*, 12 (Summer, 1975), pp. 26-36. Rpt. in *Explorations in Modern Indo-English Fiction*, ed. R.K. Dhawan. New Delhi: Bahri, 1982.

"Timid Movement of a Wing." *The Indian Literary Review* (August 1978), pp. 11-13.

"Within and Without Tradition." *ACLALS Newsletter*, 5 April 1979, pp. 5-21.

"Memoirs of a Mendicant Professor." (A Review) *Quest*, 66 (July-Sept. 1970).

"Out of the Shadows." *Indian Express*, June 10, 1984.

(vi) Interviews/Questionnaire

"Reply to the Questionnaire." *Kakatiya Journal of English Studies*, 3 (1978), pp. 1-6.

"An Interview with Anita Desai," by Yashodhara Dalmia. *The Times of India*, 29 April 1979.

"Anita Desai: Interviewed," by Jasbir Jain. *Rajasthan University Studies in English*, 12 (1979), pp. 61-69.

"An Interview with Anita Desai," by Atma Ram. *World Literature Written in English*, 16, No. 1 (November 1977), pp. 95-104. Reprinted in *Interviews with Indian English Writers*. Atma Ram. Calcutta: Writers Workshop, 1983.

"Tremendous Changes." Interview by Sunil Seth. *India Today*, December 1-15, 1980.

"Anita Desai at Work: An Interview," by Ramesh K. Srivastava. *Perspectives on Anita Desai*, ed. Ramesh K. Srivastava. Ghaziabad: Vimal, 1984.

"It's Fatal to Write with an Audience in Mind," An Interview by Ketaki Sheth. *Imprint* (June 1984).

## II. SECONDARY SOURCES

### (i) Critical Material on Anita Desai

#### (a) Books/Anthologies

Belliappa, Meena. *Anita Desai: A Study of Her Fiction.* Calcutta: Writers Workshop, 1971.

Jain, Jasbir. *Stairs to the Attic: The Novels of Anita Desai.* Jaipur: Printwell, 1987.

Prasad, Madhusudan. *Anita Desai: The Novelist.* Allahabad: New Horizon, 1981.

Rao, B. Ramachandra. *The Novels of Anita Desai.* New Delhi: Kalyani, 1977.

Sharma, R.S. *Anita Desai.* New Delhi: Arnold Heinemann, 1981.

Srivastava, Ramesh K., ed. *Perspectives on Anita Desai.* Ghaziabad: Vimal, 1984.

#### (b) Articles/Essays/Reviews

Acharya, Shanta. "Problems of the Self in the Novels of Anita Desai." *Explorations in Modern Indo-English Fiction*, ed. R.K. Dhawan. New Delhi: Bahri, 1982, pp. 236-54.

Aithal, S. Krishnamoorthy and Rashmi Aithal. "East-West Encounter in Four Indo-English Novels." *ACLALS Bulletin*, Sixth Series, No. 1 (November 1982), pp. 1-16.

Alcock, Peter. "Rope, Serpent, Fire: The Recent Fiction of Anita Desai." *Journal of Indian Writing in English*, Vol. IX, No. 1, Jan. 81, pp. 15-34.

Alladi, Uma. "To Accept or Reject: The Woman as Wife." *The Literary Criterion*, Vol. XX, No. 4, 1985, pp. 79-90.

Asnani, Shyam M. "Anita Desai's Fiction: A New Dimension." *Indian Literature*, 24, 2, March-April 1981, pp. 44-54.

——. "Theme of Withdrawal and Loneliness in Anita Desai's *Fire on the Mountain.*" *Journal of Indian Writing in English*, Vol. IX, No. 1, Jan. 81, pp. 81-92.

——. "Anita Desai: The Novelist with Unique Personal Vision." *Contemporary Indian Thought*, Vol. 14, No. 1, Jan.-March 1974, pp. 6-9, 16-21.

Bannerjee, Purabi. "Bookworm's Progress." *Statesman*, 10 April 1983.

Daftry, Nayana. "Review of *Cry, the Peacock*." *Quest*, Vol. 10, No. 1, Winter, 1983, p. 50.

Daruwalla, Keki N. "Built on a Non-issue." Review of *In Custody*. *The Hindustan Times*, 13 Jan. 1985.

Dua, M.R. "Anita Desai." *Femina*, 4 Jan. 1974, p. 25.

Dubashi, Jagannath. "*The Village by the Sea*: An Indian Family Story: Review." *India Today*, 15 April 1983.

Dult, Charmazel, "Past and Present: A Journey to Confrontation." *Journal of Indian Writing in English*, Vol. IX, No. 1, 1981, pp 67-73.

Gabriele, A. "Anita Desai's *Fire on the Mountain*. A Review." *Times Literary Supplement*, 17 June 1977, p. 721.

——. "Dreams in Old Delhi." *Times Literary Supplement*, 5, Sept. 1980, p. 948.

Ganguli, Chandra. "*Fire on the Mountain*: An Analysis." *Critical Quarterly*, 6 (Dec. 1981), pp. 43-44.

Goyal, Bhagwat S. "The World of Women Novelists." *The Hindustan Times Weekly*, Vol. 4, No. 12, Jan. 69, pp. 64-69.

Glendinning, Victoria. "Mood Indigo," Review of *Games at Twilight and Other Stories*. *Times Literary Supplement*, 1978, p. 973.

Hashima, A. "Review of *Clear Light of Day*." *International Fiction*, 1963, pp. 99-101.

Hope, Mary. "Review of Anita Desai's *Games at Twilight*." *Spectator*, 22 July 1978, p. 24.

Iyengar, K.R.S. "A Note on Anita Desai's Novels." *Banasthali Patrika*, 4 (January 1969), pp. 64-69.

Jain, Jasbir. "Anita Desai." *Indian English Novelists*, ed. Madhusudan Prasad. New Delhi: Sterling, 1982, pp. 23-50.

——. "The Use of Fantasy in Anita Desai's Novels." *Explorations in Modern Indo-English Fiction*, ed. R.K. Dhawan. New Delhi: Bahri, 1982, pp. 227-37.

Jain, Madhu. "Anita Desai: Pretty Flower in a Waste Land." *New Delhi*, 24 Nov. 1980, pp. 81-82.

Jain, Sunita. "Review of *A Village by the Sea*." *Indian Book Chronicle*: *News Reviews*, Vol. VIII, Jan.-Dec. 1983.

Jamkhandi, Sudhakar Ratnakar. "Artistic Effects of the Shifts in Point of View in Anita Desai's *Cry, the Peacock*." *Journal of Indian Writing in English*, Vol. IX, No. 1, Jan. 81, pp. 35-46.

——."Old Delhi Revisited: Anita Desai's *Clear Light of Day*," *Commonwealth Fiction*, ed. R.K. Dhawan. Classical: 1988, vol. I, pp. 245-53.

Joshi, Mukta. "Social Problems in Post Independence Indo-Anglian Fiction with Particular Reference to Women Writers." Avadh University, Ph. D.

King, Francis. "Misfortunes of a Fau." *Spectator*, 20 Oct. 1984, pp. 35-36.

Kohli, Suresh. "Indian Women Novelists in English." *Times Weekly*, Nov. 1970, p. 3.

Krishna, Francine E. "A Lulled Life." Review of *Where Shall We Go This Summer ? Quest*, No. 99, Jan-Feb. 1976, pp. 90-91.

——."Anita Desai: *Fire on the Mountain*," *Indian Literature*, Vol. 25, No. 5, Sept.-Oct. 1982, pp. 58-69.

Krishnaswamy, Shantha. "Anita Desai—The Sexist Nature of Sanity." *The Woman in Indian Fiction in English* (1950-80). New Delhi: Ashish Publishing House, 1982.

Kumar, Shiv K. "The Fiction of Anita Desai: Another View." *The Humanities Review*, 3, July-December 1981, pp. 43-46.

Lal, P. "Review of *Voices in the City*." *Littcrit*, Vol. 2, No. 2, Dec. 1976, pp. 51-53.

——."Review of *Cry, the Peacock*." *Nagpur Times*, 15 Dec. 1968.

——."Review of *Cry the Peacock*." *Times Literary Supplement*, No. 3, 182, Friday, 22 Feb. 1963.

Lee, Hermoine. "Philosophical Guerrillas." Review of Anita Desai's *Games at Twilight*. *The Observer* 13 August 1978, p. 21.

Maini, D.S. "Achievement of Anita Desai." *Indo-English Literature*, ed. K.K. Sharma. Ghaziabad: Vimal, 1977, pp. 215-30.

——. "*Cry the Peacock* as a Poetic Novel." *English Literature of the Past Fifty Years, 1917-67*, ed. C.D. Narasimhaiah. Mysore: University of Mysore, 1970, pp. 225-34.

Malhotra, M.J. "Anita Desai: A Writer with a Promise." *Bridges of Literature*. Ajmer: Sunanda Publications, 1971, pp. 205-22.

Masilamani, J.G. "Feminism in Anita Desai." *Kakatiya Journal of English Studies*, 3 (1978), pp. 25-33.

Melwani, Murli Das. "Short Stories of Anita Desai." *Economic Times*, 29 April 1979, pp. 4-6.

Mukherjee, Meenakshi, "The Theme of Displacement in Anita Desai and Kamala Markandaya." *World Literature Written in English*, 17, No. 1 (April 1978), pp. 225-35.

——. Review of *Bye-Bye, Blackbird*. *Quest*, 75 (March-April 1972), pp. 96-99.

——. *Considerations*. New Delhi: Allied, 1977.

——. "A Broader View," Review of *In Custody*. *The Indian Express*, 7 Oct. 1984.

Nissen, Foy. "A Review of *Voices in the City*." *Quest*, 48 (Jan.-March 1966), pp. 108-10.

Pande, Mrinal. "Women Without Men." Review of *Fire on the Mountain*. *The Times of India*, 18 Dec. 1977, p. 1.

Parasuram, Laxmi. "*Mountain*: A New Dimension of Feminine Self-Perception." *Literary Criterion*, Vol. XVI, No. 3, 1981, pp. 58-64.

Politt, Katha. "*Fire on the Mountain*: A Review." *New York Times Book Review*, 20 Nov. 1977.

Prasad, Hari Mohan. "Sound or Sense: A Study of Anita Desai's *Bye-Bye, Blackbird*." *Journal of Indian Writing in English*, Vol IX, No. 1, Jan. 1981, pp. 51-66

Prasad, Madhusudan, "*Where Shall We Go This Summer?* A Critical Study." *Rajasthan Journal of English Studies*, 13-14, 1981, pp. 62-68.

Rahi, R.P. "Review of *The Village by the Sea*." *Indian and Foreign Review*, 1-15 Sept. 1983.

Rai, Rameshwar. "R.K. Narayan and Anita Desai: A Study of Styles in Fictional Structures." University of Bihar, Ph. D.

Rao, A Ramakrishna. "Anita Desai's Modernist Novel." *The Literary Endeavour*, Vol. II, 2 and 3, pp. 11-14.

Rao, B. Ramachandra. "Anita Desai: Themes and Variations in the Novels and Short Stories of Anita Desai." *Journal of Literature and Aesthetics*, Vol. II, No. 2 and 3, 1982, pp. 74-79.

Rao, A.V. Krishna. "*Village by the Sea*: A Review." *Journal of Indian Writing in English*, 2, No. 2, July 1983.

Rao, Maithili. "Landscape of the Mind." *Eve's Weekly*, 6 August 1983, pp. 52-55.

Rao, Vimala. "*Where Shall We Go This Summer?* An Analysis." *Commonwealth Quarterly*, Vol. 3, No. 9, Dec. 1978.

——. "Four Women Novelists and their Concern with the Indian Element." *Journal of Mysore University* (Humanities), Summer 1965, pp. 8-16.

Ram, Atma. "Anita Desai." *Journal of Indian Writing in English*, 5, No. 2 (July 1977), pp. 39-42.

——. "*Where Shall We Go This Summer?*" *World Literature Written in English*, 15, No. 2, Nov. 1976, pp. 381-83.

——. "Anita Desai: Exploration of Inner Sensibility." *Perspective*, July 1978, pp. 54-55.

——. "Indians Slow to Recognise Talent in their Midst." *The Tribune*, 26 June 1977.

——. "Island on the Island." A review of *Where Shall We Go This Summer? World Literature Written in English*, Nov. 1977, pp. 381-83.

——. "A View of *Where Shall We Go This Summer?*" *The Journal of Indian Writing in English*, 9, No. 1, January 1981, pp. 74-80; rpt. *Response: Recent Revelations of Indian Fiction in English*, ed. Hari Mohan Prasad. Bareilly: Prakash Book Depot, 1983, pp. 241-48.

—— "Shiv K. Kumar and Anita Desai: New Dimension to Indian English Fiction." *Triveni*, Jan.-March 1984, pp. 32-37.

Rao, Shyamala B. "Women Writers in Indo-Anglian Fiction." *Century*, 26 Jan. 1972, pp. 25-34.

Ray, Karen. "*Clear ight of Day*: A Review." *Christian Science Monitor*, 28 Jan. 1981, p. 17.

Reuben, Elizabeth. "Anita Desai's *Fire on the Mountain*." *World Literature Written in English*, 17, No. 1, April 1978, pp 234-36.

Sethi. Sunil. "Pieces of the Past." Review of Anita Desai's *Clear Light of Day*. *India Today*, 5, No. 23, December 1-15, 1980, pp. 142-43.

Sharma, D.R. "Anita Desai." *The Tribune*, 2 April 1978.

Sharma, R.S. "Alienation, Accommodation and the Locale in Anita Desai's *Bye-Bye, Blackbird*." *Literary Criterion*, Vol. 14, No. 4, 1979, pp. 31-49.

——. "Movement and Stillness in Anita Desai's *Fire on the Mountain*." *Littcrit*, Vol. 4, No. 2, Dec. 1978, pp. 1-6.

——. "Mother and the City: Archetypes in Anita Desai's *Voices in the City*." *Journal of Literary Studies*, Vol. 2, No. 2, Dec. 1979, pp. 57-77.

Shastri, N.R. "*Where Shall We Go This Summer ?* : A Critical Study." *Osmania Journal of English Studies*, Vol. 17, 1981, pp. 83-103.

Singh, Brij Raj. "The Fiction of Anita Desai." *The Humanities Review*, 3, No. 2 (July-December 1981), pp. 40-43.

Singh, C.P. "The Visitor and the Exile: A Study in Anita Desai's *Bye-Bye, Blackbird*." *Response: Recent Revelations of Indian Fiction in English*, ed. Hari Mohan Prasad. Bareilly: Prakash Book Depot, 1983.

Singh, R.S. "Aloneness Alone: Anita Desai and Arun Joshi." *Indian Novel in English*. New Delhi: Arnold Heinemann, 1977, pp. 164-77.

Sivaramakrishna. "From Alienation to Mythic Acceptance: The Ordeal of Consciousness in Anita Desai's Fiction." *Kakatiya Journal of English Studies*, 3, No. 1, 1978, pp. 7-24.

Srivastava, Ramesh K. "Voices of Artists in the City." *Journal of Indian Writing in English*, Vol. IX, No. 1, Jan. 1981, pp. 47-57.

Stewart, Ian. "Recent Fiction." Review of Anita Desai's *Games at Twilight. Illustrated London News*, October 1978, p. 120.

Sunwani, V.K. "Carignano—A Quiet place." *Journal of Literary Studies*, 2, No. 2, Dec. 1979, pp. 79-92.

T. Vijay Kumar. Review of *In Custody. Indian Book Chronicle*, 10, Nos. 17-18, Sept. 1-10, 1985, pp. 286-87.

Varady, Evelyn. "American and British Responses and Anita Desai's *Games at Twilight and Other Stories*." *Journal of Indian Writing in English*, 8, Nos. 1-2, Jan.-July 1982, pp. 27-34.

Vyas, B.O. "Vivid Voices of the Inner Kingdom." *Journal of Indian Writing in English*, Vol. IV, No. 1. Jan. 1981, pp. 1-14.

Weir, Ann Lowry. "The Illusion of Maya: Feminine Consciousness in Anita Desai's *Cry, the Peacock*." *Journal of South Asian Literature*, 21, No. 2, Summer-Fall 1981, pp. 1-41.

——. "Anita Desai: *Fire on the Mountain*." *World Literature Written in English*, 17, No. 2, Nov. 1978, pp. 548-50.

Wiehe, Janet. "*Clear Light of Day*: A Review." *Library Journal*, 1 Oct. 1980.

## (ii) Critical Material on Third Force Psychology and its application

Fromm, Erich. *The Art of Loving*. 1957; rpt. London: Unwin, 1976.

——. *Escape From Freedom*. New York: Rinehart, 1941.

——. *The Fear of Freedom*. 1942; rpt. London: Routledge and Kegan Paul, 1960.

Horney, Karen. *Feminine Psychology*, ed. Harold Kalman. New York: Norton, 1967.

——. *Neurosis and Human Growth: The Struggle Toward Self-Realization*. 1951; rept. London: Routlege and Kegan Paul, 1965.

——. *The Neurotic Personality of Our Time.* New York: Norton, 1937.

——. *New Ways in Psychoanalysis.* New York: Norton, 1939.

——. "On Feeling Abused." *American Journal of Psychoanalysis*, 11 (1951), pp. 5-12. Rpt. in Kelman, 1964, pp. 29-46, and Rubins, 1972, pp. 97-103.

——. *Our Inner Conflicts: A Constructive Theory of Neurosis.* New York: Norton, 1945.

——. "The Paucity of Inner Experiences." *American Journal of Psychoanalysis*, 12 (1952), pp. 3-9. Rpt. in Kelman, 1964, pp. 47-64, and Rubins, 1972, pp. 97-103.

——. *Self-Analysis.* New York: Norton, 1942.

——. "The Value of Vindictiveness." *American Journal of Psychoanalysis*, 8 (1948), pp. 3-12. Rpt. in Kelman, 1965, pp.27-51.

——., ed. *Are You Considering Psychoanalysis ?* New York: Norton, 1946.

Paris, Bernard J. "Bargains with Fate: A Psychological Approach to Shakespeare's Major Tragedies." *The Aligarh Journal of English Studies*, 5 (1980), pp. 144-61.

——. "Bargains with Fate: The Case of Macbeth." *American Journal of Psychoanalysis*, 42 (1982), pp. 7-20.

——. *Character and Conflict in Jane Austen's Novels: A Psychological Approach.* Detroit: Wayne State Univ. Press, 1978; Brighton: Harvester Press, 1979.

——. "Experience of Thomas Hardy." In *The Victorian Experience: The Novelists*, ed. Richard A. Levine. Athens: Ohio Univ. Press, 1976, pp. 203-37.

——. "Hamlet and His Problems: A Horneyan Analysis." *The Centennial Review*, 21 (1977), pp. 36-66.

——. "Horney's Theory and the Study of Literature." *American Journal of Psychoanalysis*, 38 (1978) pp. 343-53.

——. " 'Hush, hush ! He's a human being': A Psychological Approach to Heathcliff." *Women and Literature*, No. 2 (1982), pp. 101-17.

——. "The Inner Conflicts of *Measure for Measure*." *The Centennial Review*, 25 (1981), pp. 266-76.

——. *A Psychological Approach to Fiction: Studies in Thackeray, Stendhal, George Eliot, Dostoevsky, and Conrad.* Bloomington: Indiana Univ. Press, 1974.

——. "Richard III: Shakespeare's First Great Mimetic Character." *The Aligarh Journal of English Studies*, 8 (1983), pp. 40-67.

——. "Third Force Psychology and the Study of Literature." *Psychological Perspectives on Literature: Freudian Dissidents and Non-Freudians, A Casebook*, ed. Joseph Natoli. Hampden, CT: Archon, 1984, pp. 155-80.

——. "The Two Selves of Rodion Raskolnikov." *Gradiva, A Journal of Contemporary Theory and Practice*, 1 (1978), pp. 316-28; garbled text on 320 corrected in 2 (1979), pp. i-ii.

# INDEX